W9-CXO-310

CONTENTS

Marry Mare

SCORPIO

1998
TOTAL HOROSCOPE
♏ OCT 23 – NOV 22 ♏

J
JOVE BOOKS, NEW YORK

Astrological perspectives by Michael Lutin

The publishers regret that they cannot
answer individual letters requesting personal
horoscope information.

1998 TOTAL HOROSCOPE: SCORPIO

PRINTING HISTORY
Jove edition/July 1997

The Putnam Berkley World Wide Web address is
http://www.berkley.com

ISBN: 0-515-12115-0

MESSAGE TO SCORPIO

Dear Scorpio,

Yours is a nature of dark intensity and swirling passions. Sexual magnetism pervades your whole being and you have a serious interest in your sex life. The rumors and myths have it that Scorpio has the best love life of all the signs, but it's not always true. Scorpios develop early and experiment in many ways emotionally when they are very young. They often have many sexual experiences in their search for an ideal mate, one who can satisfy their intense needs. When they find one, they are faithful, honorable, and usually monogamous. However, love life can be a problem. Scorpios may have to rechannel their drives and fit them into realistic life patterns, effecting a total change.

But the passion for life never dies. No matter what your private life is like, you have a thirst for love and a desire for survival that makes you irresistible. Sometimes, when people hear you're Scorpio, they act a little afraid. It's usually a ruse to cover up their titillation and excitement and secret hope that you'll seduce them. You are stirred by primitive passions that are the basis for your sexual orientation, creative drives, and need for self-expression. No other sign has such a profound instinct for survival and reproduction. Out of the abyss of your emotions come a thousand creations, each one with a life of its own, each one like an incomprehensible abstract painting.

So you are a passionate lover and a prolific artist. Often your eyes snap and crackle with the dark energy of your whole being. When you fix your interest on someone or something, you become obsessed.

Nothing, but nothing, can stop you from winning your lover or achieving your goal. You are competitive and determined, fortified with enough endurance and stamina to outlive any enemy, physical or psychological. When challenged you can spit in the eye of death and pursue your ambitions despite every threat, warning, or obstacle in your path. You simply cannot be deterred. You know when to wait. When you smell danger, you retreat into a cave. Your eyes peer out of the darkness. You count your losses and recoup your strength. When the moment is right you reemerge, stronger than ever, healed and invincible.

You are friendly, considerate, and generous. Your strength and courage are inspiring qualities that people around you admire and call upon when they are in trouble. You are fiercely loyal and don't like anyone to fool around with your mate. You're jealous, possessive, and dangerously aroused if you think people are taking advantage of you. You prefer not to fight openly because you know how bloody the battle can get. You are not afraid to fight, however, and your life is often intensely gripped in life-and-death situations. You remain in a constant state of readiness and awareness, like an animal that sleeps with one eye open.

When the fight is actually on, you'll do what is necessary to win. You'll be devious, ruthless, and cruel. You'll save a bitter, sarcastic remark for the right moment, then hit your opponent with a barb that pierces deep and strikes its deathly blow. In this sense you have a cold streak. You keep your emotions under control, then act quickly and decisively in any situation that calls for striking while the iron is hot.

Sometimes you smell danger when it isn't there, which causes trouble in many of your relationships. You are cautious, suspicious, and deeply aware of your position with respect to other people. When you think there's a threat, you can become vindictive, treacherous, and filled with venom.

But isn't all this a little dramatic? Frankly, yes. Scorpios' actual lives are not smoldering and steeping like volcanoes and jungles. Most of the time you lead simple, normal lives. You work, raise families, have relationships, keep house. But Scorpio's dramatic intensity is there nonetheless. Creative self-expression is a must. Without it, you will create intrigues and complexities or work all that energy back in on yourself as illness or disease.

You are an ardent and faithful lover—there is no doubt about that. When you are truly in love you can be tender, compassionate, forgiving. Otherwise, sex can be a selfish and shallow affair. In some areas of your life, you cut people out without a thought and never forget wrongs that are done to you. But on the whole, you don't like to lose touch or control of those you love. People can be just as shocked by your greed as they are excited by it. You have to develop a spiritual side if you are not to get lost in self-indulgence and materialistic pursuits.

You are a hardheaded realist. You are generous with your belongings provided there's enough for you. For those you love you are a divine provider. Anything they want, you are prepared to offer. You delight in satisfying their desires. When it comes to money, you are generally lucky. You believe in luck and because you do, it happens to you. You are certainly not an idler who sits around hoping for the best. When you want something, you are ambitious, persistent, thorough, efficient, and hardworking. But you believe in an overall luck in finances, and as a result you rarely go without. You often rise to great heights, financially or otherwise, because you unite drive and magnetism. It's hard for people to resist or refuse you.

You are often suspicious of those around you. Either your siblings posed some limitation on you which you had to conquer, or some adolescent problem made you grow up and look at the world through the eyes of a determined realist. Whatever the original cause, the result is your amazing power to perceive people for what they are. Your capacity for penetrating analysis is unsurpassable. It will be of help to you in any creative career field.

You generally don't want to be tied down to home and family, although your primitive territorial instincts often drive you toward claiming a partner and mating. You don't want your domestic scene to be a humdrum, run-of-the-mill one, and often you set a scandalous example for your neighbors to follow.

You're a strict parent who is often undone by your kids. It's hard for children to understand your single-minded, often rough demeanor. You are sometimes caught between your need to satisfy the desires of your ego and your responsibilities to the youngsters. This can lead to guilt, deception, and disillusion which can only be resolved by time and maturity.

No matter what you're involved in, you can be a ferocious fanatic. You can work like a fiend, especially on projects that are new and exciting and that tap your creativity, originality, and inventiveness. You're naturally sound of body and of a strong, healthy constitution. You can imagine the worst, because you're a person of extremes—extreme highs and lows, extreme obsessions, extreme fantasies. Although you possess remarkable physical endurance and resilience, you tend to magnify your ills and, through worry, aggravate them. Your sex organs, intestines, and organs of elimination are vitally connected with all your other glands and your body in general. By reflex you are physically joined to the throat, spine, heart, and circulatory system. Physical and psychic functions are united through your glands. Acceptance of your sexual identity is one key to health and success.

You can draw the best and richest resources out of

people. In your relationships you can be parasitic or inspiring; you can take life or give it. You tend to marry for money or to enrich your life somehow. Your best partners are conservative, gentle, faithful, honorable, firm—lovers who will support you on any level. You need someone who loves pleasure and can see you through brooding and bad moods. You can provide a strong sense of renewal and transformation for your partner. Your arrival may mark a permanent revision in your mate's life, the closing of some doors forever and the opening of new ones.

Your sexual experimentalism is a usual part of your development. Your ethical standards are traditional. But your baser interest in superficial, even tawdry sex, contradicts your need for stable, monogamous relationships and high moral codes. The religious principles of your ancestors often play a role in your life. So you must come to terms with the philosophical teachings of your childhood while striking out on your own to find yourself.

You are a proud, noble creature whose aim is to shine and be great at whatever you do. You need the spotlight. Show business and sports attract you. You look up to people who sparkle and express their creative selves with flair and style. Style is something you've got plenty of yourself. You like to look good, and you project yourself with flair and drama. You're a great host and entertainer. But you are a creature of the night with a great need for intimacy, secrecy, and intrigue. You are often outgoing, helpful, and friendly, a humble and earnest servant to your friends. You strive for honor above all things. Yet it is often said—and rightly so—that a Scorpio never tells everything. There are things about you no one will ever know. They may be simple, unimportant, silly things, but they're all yours.

You may look to someone around you for direction, money, focus, or criticism, but basically you are a self-directed creature with a will of steel. Relationships, both personal and professional, often haunt you, because you chase and run away from them at the same time. You need another human being desperately. You long to lock horns on the battlefield of love and sex, and your desire and passion for the touch of a loving hand are hungers you cannot escape. You have a burning desire to create life, to deliver yourself into another human being's love. But it's hard for you to surrender your identity to another, so you collide and flee, only to be drawn again into contact. This obsessiveness forces you to reexamine yourself and your desire for an intimate relationship.

You are a dominant figure who makes an excellent partner. You will is strong and your demands are great. You like to rule, loathe criticism, and seek always to be the master of the situation. Although you manipulate and control, and operate on all levels at once—conscious and unconscious—you are a dauntless hero with a magician's touch for turning away evil.

You are attracted to mystery with a bloodhound's nose for solving it. No clues escape your scrutiny. No suspects elude your penetrating gaze and analytical mind. You are a fearsome adversary, an eloquent cross-examiner. When you sniff out a lead, you're on the track and never rest till the case is solved.

Your problems are always solved with one pure quality: strength of purpose. You can blind your eyes to facts and latch on to fantastic obsessions, unrealistic schemes, and impossible desires. Your rigid stamina and unshakable faith often lead you to victory anyway. But there are moments when you're down and nobody can pull you out of the mud of your own depressions. Loving partners may try, but you may strike out at them and send them away. Nobody can save you from yourself at these times, except you. When you come to the conclusion that something is bad for you, you can eradicate it swiftly from your life, painlessly and forever, without blinking twice. But it takes you a while to get to that point, because you like to pass endurance tests.

Of all the Scorpio traits, there is one that is most inspiring. It is the quality of personality that sets you apart and makes you the extraordinary creature you are. It makes you the bravest of all your astrological cousins and puts you in a category with mystics and magicians of all ages. This is the Scorpio capacity for total transformation—what is termed metamorphosis.

You may have read somewhere that there are two types of Scorpio—the scorpion and the eagle.

The scorpion is capable of biting itself and dying from its own venom. So watch out for your baser instincts of revenge and bitterness. But there is honor and nobility in the scorpion's nature. If you try to escape from your animal self and pretend it isn't there, it's possible that you will poison your whole system. The animal drives get the credit for that remarkable instinct you have for survival—the driving, unintelligent, uncommunicating, unthinking reaction to danger that makes you win in battle. The thirst for power is the danger here. Nobody is more capable of being carried away with power than Scorpio. Your instinct for survival could be magnified into a power hunger that would never stop, and you could go on drawing life from all who came near. Eventually you could engulf yourself in greed, desire, and lust, and even draw life from yourself.

The eagle is reputed to be the symbol of nobility. The bird flies over all, a transformed being representative of the higher side of Scorpio, the healer and magician. Scorpio has battled the forces of darkness and death, and won. He has confronted the illusions of danger and self-annihilation, and emerged supreme. Nothing frightens him because he has pierced his own fears and fantasies. He has faced himself and passed the ultimate test. He is the embodiment of truth and lives to heal the wounds of his fellow man. Fear and disease flee from him, for he has proved himself against visions and manifestations of evil. He has successfully and consciously survived personal crisis. Now he has wings on high in joyous celebration of victory.

But again, all this sounds a bit heavy and dramatic. You don't really live in such tempestuous, mysterious existences, do you? Or do you? Scorpio wrestles with forces beyond the visible world, parts of the consciousness that are the outposts of the mind. Even if such battles are going on, how do you change from one kind of Scorpio to another? Is that kind of total change possible for anybody?

Yes. You are the one who can make the change more than anyone else. Scorpio has the capacity of the caterpillar to spin its own cocoon. You just spin and spin without knowing what will happen, if anything. You enter the cocoon consciously, willingly, facing the end of one existence without knowing anything about what lies ahead. All you have is the fact that you are alive and conscious and gifted with some brilliant something we will call intelligence. You have to have the courage to say good-bye to your old way of life, safe and sure and happy though it was, and step into that cocoon, and spin it shut right to the top. At that point nothing comes in. Nothing goes out. The past is over. For all intents and purposes everything seems dead.

Then amid the vacuum of uncertainty, from the darkness of doubt and dread, the cocoon is broken. Something has occurred. Can we call it miraculous? This is the meaning of Scorpio. From the hopelessness of despair and the inevitability of personal crisis, transformation can be achieved.

                                            Michael Lutin

SCORPIO SNEAK PREVIEW
OF THE 21st CENTURY

As the last decade of the twentieth century comes to a close, planetary aspects for its final years connect you with the future. Major changes completed in 1995 and 1996 form the bridge to the twenty-first century and new horizons. The years 1997 through 1999 and into the year 2000 reveal hidden paths and personal hints for achieving your potential, your message from the planets.

Scorpio individuals, ruled by the planets Pluto and Mars, have been enjoying a long period of experimentation, change, and rejuvenation. Pluto, the planet of beginnings and endings, in its own home in Scorpio through November 1995, has enabled you to leap ahead in understanding and tolerance. Emotional expression and spiritual values, undergoing transformation, underscore all material considerations. As Pluto in Scorpio completes one cycle of growth, Pluto in Sagittarius takes you on a new journey of exploration and learning.

Pluto is in Sagittarius late 1995 to the year 2007. Sagittarius, ruled by good-luck planet Jupiter, is the sign of education, philosophy, and religion, of expansiveness, risk, and gambling. Optimistic Sagittarius and enduring Scorpio combine to produce a vibrant life force. While Sagittarius exuberantly encourages taking chances, Scorpio shrewdly calculates the odds and plots strategy. When Sagittarius broadens the horizon, Scorpio imbues new experiences with deep meaning.

The urge to take chances in love and money are stimulated by Jupiter, which also provides protection and lucky breaks. Such chances have potential for fortunate outcomes through Saturn, planet of reason and responsibility, which rules Capricorn and Aquarius. With Saturn's wise and disciplined influence, what you sow you are likely to reap.

Jupiter in Capricorn all 1996 to early 1997 provides a conservative base for planning and building. Jupiter in Aquarius 1997 to early 1998 secures the future through intellectual output and worthy service. Jupiter is in Pisces, an excellent aspect to your own Sun and Pluto, 1998 to early 1999. With Jupiter in fluid Pisces, inspiration flows over all your undertakings.

Saturn in Aries spring 1996 to early 1999 and Jupiter in Aries 1999 to March 2000 are also in good aspect to your Sun and Pluto. Saturn and Jupiter in fiery Aries tap your iron energy and steely endurance at the forge of success where you can hammer out cherished goals. Saturn enters Taurus March 1999 for a three-year stay. Because Taurus is your zodiacal partner as well as your zodiacal opposite, there is stability mixed with challenge as one century ends and a new century begins.

Taking chances also has great potential with Uranus and Neptune. Uranus, planet of innovation, sparks Scorpio powers of healing change. Uranus is in Aquarius early 1996 to the year 2003. Neptune, planet of vision and mystery, is most compatible with the Scorpio love of investigation and creativity. Neptune in Capricorn through late November 1998 inspires a wealth of creative research, lending practicality to your imagination. Neptune enters Aquarius late 1998 and remains in Aquarius to the year 2011.

Both Uranus and Neptune in Aquarius as the century turns send strong currents through your tough magnetic core, turning your mind and heart on to the mysteries of life. When the idealism of Pluto in Sagittarius joins the dynamism of Scorpio, you are justified in taking chances. Follow Pluto, your rising star. With its power to change your life completely, all your efforts build to an exciting finish.

THE CUSP-BORN SCORPIO

Are you *really* a Scorpio? If your birthday falls during the third to fourth week of October, at the beginning of Scorpio, will you still retain the traits of Libra, the sign of the Zodiac before Scorpio? What if you were born late in November—are you more Sagittarius than Scorpio? Many people born at the edge, or cusp, of a sign have difficulty determining exactly what sign they are. If you are one of these people, here's how you can figure it out, once and for all.

Consult the table on page 17. Find the year you were born, and then note the day. The table will tell you the precise days on which the Sun entered and left your sign for the year of your birth. If you were born at the beginning or end of Scorpio, yours is a lifetime reflecting a process of subtle transformation. Your life on Earth will symbolize a significant change in consciousness, for you are either about to enter a whole new way of living or you are leaving one behind.

If you were born at the beginning of Scorpio, you may want to read the horoscope book for Libra as well as Scorpio, for Libra holds the keys to much of the complexity of your spirit and reflects many of your hidden weaknesses, secret sides, and unspoken wishes.

You have a keen way of making someone feel needed and desired, whether you care deeply or not. Sex is a strong directive in your life. You might turn your charm and seductiveness toward gaining a merely superficial relationship. You could use your sexual magnetism and love magic to win people over for the sheer purpose of being seen as partnered in a respectable couple.

You can love with an almost fatal obsession, a bigger-than-both-of-you type thing. You may blind your eyes to basic incompatibilities just to keep the peace in a relationship—then suddenly declare war.

No one in the whole Zodiac is as turned on to the passions of life as you are. You can survive any crisis, for deep in your spirit lie the seeds of immortality and you know it. Above all you are the symbol that life goes on—the personification of awakening passion.

If you were born at the end of Scorpio, you may want to read the horoscope book for Sagittarius as well as Scorpio. You are the symbol of the human mind awakening to its higher capabilities. What you are leaving behind is greed, blind desire, and shallow lust, as you awaken to your own ability to learn, to create, and to understand.

You want to travel, see new places, see how people live, figure yourself out, acquire knowledge—yet you are often not quite ready to take the plunge. When you shift your behavior patterns significantly and permanently, new worlds open up and you turn on to immortality and the infinite possibilities of your own mind.

THE CUSPS OF SCORPIO

DATES SUN ENTERS SCORPIO
(LEAVES LIBRA)

October 23 every year from 1900 to 2000,
except for the following:

October 22	October 24			
1992	1902	1911	1923	1943
96	03	14	27	47
	06	15	31	51
	07	18	35	55
	10	19	39	59

DATES SUN LEAVES SCORPIO
(ENTERS SAGITTARIUS)

November 22 every year from 1900 to 2000,
except for the following:

November 21		November 23		
1976	1992	1902	1915	1931
80	93	03	19	35
84	96	07	23	39
88		10	27	43
		11		

SCORPIO RISING:
YOUR ASCENDANT

Could you be a "double" Scorpio? That is, could you have Scorpio as your Rising sign as well as your Sun sign? The tables on pages 20–21 will tell you Scorpios what your Rising sign happens to be. Just find the hour of your birth, then find the day of your birth, and you will see which sign of the Zodiac is your Ascendant, as the Rising sign is called.

Your Ascendant, or Rising sign, modifies your basic Sun sign personality, and it affects the way you act out the daily predictions for your Sun sign. If your Rising sign is indeed Scorpio, what follows is a description of its effects on your horoscope. If your Rising sign is some other sign of the Zodiac, you may wish to read the horoscope book for that sign as well.

With Scorpio Rising, look to planets Mars and Pluto, the rulers of Scorpio. You have the tremendous energy of Mars and the implacable avenging power of Pluto, which together make you a tower of forcefulness. Mars accentuates action, Pluto signifies spiritual development. You can be a bold crusader for truth, a relentless foe of injustice. Or you can be bitter, sarcastic, vengeful, and capable of harboring destructive impulses toward the self as well as toward society.

There may be dramatic extremes in the conduct of your life. You will obsessively pursue a goal, be consumed by it, seemingly drop it, then move on to a new sphere of endeavor and influence. Pluto, the planet of transformation, emphasizes beginnings and endings in a continuum of development. The marked variations in your lifestyle may be an expression of that cycle of change. Your capacity to learn from experience is immense, and this ability enables you to rise to great positions during a lifetime.

Control is a byword for Scorpio Rising. Whether it is control over self, control over others, or control through others, you are a great strategist. In your arsenal are such contradictory traits as subtlety, intensity, selfishness, self-sacrifice, ruthlessness, possessiveness, aloofness, impulsiveness, determination. Linked to your need for control is your love of power. You have enough passion and endurance to attain power, and then to use it to change your environment.

As much as you like to dominate, you hate being dominated. You will go to great lengths to escape being trapped in a chafing relationship or situation. People may see you as perverse and self-seeking, ready for flight or fight. You hate to lose, whether the conquest is an argument, or a cause, or a lover. Your anger and jealousy are renowned. You get deeply involved, though your manner can be impersonal. You have a penchant for solitude and secrecy, so people often think you are introverted and shy—until they get to know you intimately.

Your potential for inner growth and external change is almost unlimited. A constantly developing spiritual component puts you in touch with the mysterious forces of the universe. Your energy and drive are rooted in the psychosexual nature of humankind, which is indeed a basic organizer of all human effort and thought. On an operational level, your initiative and inventiveness give you a practical side that often obscures the depths of your being.

Stamina and transformation are key words for Scorpio Rising. You can change situations for good or bad, for selfless service or self-promotion. You can lead the struggle for survival and creativity.

RISING SIGNS FOR SCORPIO

Hour of Birth*	Day of Birth		
	October 23–27	October 28–31	November 1–5
Midnight	Leo	Leo	Leo
1 AM	Leo	Leo; Virgo 10/30	Virgo
2 AM	Virgo	Virgo	Virgo
3 AM	Virgo	Virgo	Virgo; Libra 11/5
4 AM	Libra	Libra	Libra
5 AM	Libra	Libra	Libra
6 AM	Libra	Libra; Scorpio 10/30	Scorpio
7 AM	Scorpio	Scorpio	Scorpio
8 AM	Scorpio	Scorpio	Scorpio
9 AM	Sagittarius	Sagittarius	Sagittarius
10 AM	Sagittarius	Sagittarius	Sagittarius
11 AM	Sagittarius	Capricorn	Capricorn
Noon	Capricorn	Carpricorn	Capricorn
1 PM	Capricorn; Aquarius 10/26	Aquarius	Aquarius
2 PM	Aquarius	Aquarius	Pisces
3 PM	Pisces	Pisces	Pisces; Aries 11/5
4 PM	Aries	Aries	Aries
5 PM	Aries; Taurus 10/26	Taurus	Taurus
6 PM	Taurus	Taurus	Gemini
7 PM	Gemini	Gemini	Gemini
8 PM	Gemini	Gemini;	Cancer
9 PM	Cancer	Cancer	Cancer
10 PM	Cancer	Cancer	Cancer
11 PM	Leo	Leo	Leo

*Hour of birth given here is for Standard Time in any time zone. If your hour of birth was recorded in Daylight Saving Time, subtract one hour from it and consult that hour in the table above. For example, if you were born at 7 AM D.S.T., see 6 AM above.

	Day of Birth		
Hour of Birth	**November 6–11**	**November 12–16**	**November 17–23**
Midnight	Leo	Leo; Virgo 11/15	Virgo
1 AM	Virgo	Virgo	Virgo
2 AM	Virgo	Virgo	Virgo; Libra 11/21
3 AM	Libra	Libra	Libra
4 AM	Libra	Libra	Libra
5 AM	Libra	Libra; Scorpio 11/14	Scorpio
6 AM	Scorpio	Scorpio	Scorpio
7 AM	Scorpio	Scorpio	Scorpio; Sagittarius 11/21
8 AM	Sagittarius	Sagittarius	Sagittarius
9 AM	Sagittarius	Sagittarius	Sagittarius
10 AM	Sagittarius	Capricorn	Capricorn
11 AM	Capricorn	Capricorn	Capricorn
Noon	Capricorn; Aquarius 11/10	Aquarius	Aquarius
1 PM	Aquarius	Aquarius	Pisces
2 PM	Pisces	Pisces	Pisces; Aries 11/21
3 PM	Aries	Aries	Aries
4 PM	Aries	Taurus	Taurus
5 PM	Taurus	Taurus	Gemini
6 PM	Gemini	Gemini	Gemini
7 PM	Gemini	Gemini; Cancer 11/16	Cancer
8 PM	Cancer	Cancer	Cancer
9 PM	Cancer	Cancer	Cancer; Leo 11/22
10 PM	Leo	Leo	Leo
11 PM	Leo	Leo	Leo

LOVE AND RELATIONSHIPS

No matter who you are, what you do in life, or where your planets are positioned, you still need to be loved, and to feel love for other human beings. Human relationships are founded on many things: infatuation, passion, sex, guilt, friendship, and a variety of other complex motivations, frequently called love.

Relationships often start out full of hope and joy, the participants sure of themselves and sure of each other's love, and then end up more like a pair of gladiators than lovers. When we are disillusioned, bitter, and wounded, we tend to blame the other person for difficulties that were actually present long before we ever met. Without seeing clearly into our own natures we will be quite likely to repeat our mistakes the next time love comes our way.

Enter Astrology.

It is not always easy to accept, but knowledge of ourselves can improve our chances for personal happiness. It is not just by predicting when some loving person will walk into our lives, but by helping us come to grips with our failures and reinforce our successes.

Astrology won't solve all our problems. The escapist will ultimately have to come to terms with the real world around him. The hard-bitten materialist will eventually acknowledge the eternal rhythms of the infinite beyond which he can see or hear. Astrology does not merely explain away emotion. It helps us unify the head with the heart so that we can become whole individuals. It helps us define what it is we are searching for, so we can recognize it when we find it.

Major planetary cycles have been changing people's ideas about love and commitment, marriage, partnerships, and relationships. These cycles have affected virtually everyone in areas of personal involvement. Planetary forces point out upheavals and transformations occurring in all of society. The concept of marriage is being totally reexamined. Exactly what the changes will ultimately bring no one can tell. It is usually difficult to determine which direction society will take. One thing is certain: no man is an island. If the rituals and pomp of wedding ceremonies must be revised, then it will happen.

Social rules are being revised. Old outworn institutions are indeed crumbling. But relationships will not die. People are putting less stress on permanence and false feelings of security. The emphasis now shifts toward the union of two loving souls. Honesty, equality, and mutual cooperation are the goals in modern marriage. When these begin to break down, the marriage is in jeopardy. Surely there must be a balance between selfish separatism and prematurely giving up.

There is no doubt that astrology can establish the degree of compatibility between two human beings. Two people can share a common horizon in life but have quite different habits or basic interests. Two others might have many basic characteristics in common while needing to approach their goals from vastly dissimilar points of view. Astrology describes compatibility based on these assumptions.

It compares and contrasts through the fundamental characteristics that draw two people together. Although they could be at odds on many basic levels, two people could find themselves drawn together again and again. Sometimes it seems that we keep being attracted to the same type of individuals. We might ask ourselves if we have learned anything from our past mistakes. The answer is that there are qualities in people that we require and thus seek out time and time again. To solve that mystery in ourselves is to solve much of the dilemma of love, and so to help ourselves determine if we are approaching a wholesome situation or a potentially destructive one.

We are living in a very curious age with respect to marriage and relationships. We can easily observe the shifting social attitudes concerning the whole institution of marriage. People are seeking everywhere for answers to their own inner needs. In truth, all astrological combinations can achieve compatibility. But many relationships seem doomed before they get off the ground. Astrologically there can be too great a difference between the goals, aspirations, and personal outlook of the people involved. Analysis of both horoscopes must and will indicate enough major planetary factors to keep the two individuals together. Call it what you will: determination, patience, understanding, love—whatever it may be, two people have the capacity to achieve a state of fulfillment together. We all have different needs and desires. When it comes to choosing a mate, you really have to know yourself. If you know the truth about what you are really looking for, it will make it easier to find. Astrology is a useful, almost essential, tool to that end.

In the next chapter your basic compatibility with each of the twelve signs of the Zodiac is generalized. The planetary vibrations between you and an individual born under any given zodiacal sign suggest much about how you will relate to each other. Hints are provided about love and romance, sex and marriage so that you and your mate can get the most out of the relationship that occupies so important a role in your life.

SCORPIO:
YOU AND YOUR MATE

SCORPIO—ARIES

This is an exciting and dangerous combination. Aries makes you work, and you turn your Aries on, deep down at the most primitive levels of being. Instead of turning these interactions against yourselves and developing a diabolical and constantly escalating war, you can work them into a source of inspiration on fundamental sexual, emotional, creative, and practical levels.

You share the primary instincts for being: survival, life, death. When it comes to ambition, energy, and stamina, you are both unbeatable. You are both stubborn and strong-willed. You conflict in your views of openness and secrecy, freedom and control. When you cooperate and step out of each other's way, it's a dynamic combination. In battle you can be a pair of warring wills, fighting it out till the bitter end.

At the same time, you can be a couple of mystical magicians. Together your powers of creativity, renewal, and regeneration can build a new world. Your collisions are explosive and exciting. The product of these eruptions could be enough light and heat to launch a thousand ships. At best, you create a deep, lasting alliance of resilience and indestructibility.

Hints for Your Aries Mate

Both of you, ruled by the fiery red planet Mars, may think that combat is the cure for being frustrated and thwarted. Wrong! You know your Aries mate will argue till dawn against your scalpel-sharp criticism. There's no winning, and as your thrust gets parried, the blade gets dulled. Of course, you must be brave and heroic in the areas where your bold Aries mate wavers. Always insist that your mate be on time for appointments, follow through on commitments, see to the details of the grand plan. Remind him or her in advance; don't wait till the mistake is made so you can heap failure on Aries. That's where the arguments start. Another area is money. Hide it, bank it, keep it away from your mate's pocket where a hole is burning. A third area is flirtation. Come down hard here, even if you have to give ultimatums. Your sex life with Aries is so magnificent, she or he will not want it threatened by any foolishness.

SCORPIO—TAURUS

Here is an exciting blend of the spiritual and the material. You both appreciate what this world has to offer and love the pleasures of this earthly life. But you are opposites after all, and harmony without opposition and conflict will be impossible. You both may feel a lightning upsurge of electricity, need for change, excitement, emotional and sexual growth, and the feeling of independence. The shock of sudden crisis and reversal, the creative challenge that awakens you to life and its meaning—the power and drives of our primitive desires—these are the keys that will unlock the future for this combination.

If you are not to go to war over every last possession or descend into the depths of self-indulgence, you will have to look for values beyond simple materialism. You're both loyal, protective, and fiercely possessive. You can be staunch friends and honorable companions. Your mutual attraction is so powerful that it would take a tremendous explosion to separate you.

Finances are an integral part of your partnership. So is sex. They can destroy your relationship, or they can enhance it. It all depends on your success in developing your values.

Hints for Your Taurus Mate

You and Taurus can be opposites or zodiacal mates, depending on what you both do with the fact that you are polarized in the astrological scheme of things. You both have a lot to learn from each other. For example, you, Scorpio, must borrow the Taurus gift of patience, cooling things out before you have to placate your mate when he or she sees red. Sometimes it is you who ruffles your mate's placid exterior with criticism and demands; that's waving the red flag in front of the Bull. Your loyalty matches that of your Taurus mate, but she or he doesn't want to wait till you've separated to learn how much you care. Have more respect for the little things your mate likes by joining them. Enjoy the ease of a comfortable home, fool around with all the gadgets, fix them without complaining. Relax with wine and food, hold hands in the movies, munching popcorn, meander home, dwelling on the pleasures you've tasted instead of delivering a high-pressure lecture about tomorrow.

SCORPIO—GEMINI

This match can surge with the new life you can sense in the air on a spring day. It can also have the sting of a swarm of bees. Together you form a blend of dark intensity and joyous frivolity. Emotionally and sexually you can be a mighty exciting pair, mutually stimulating primitive passions with a light humorous approach to sex and life. This relationship will surely cover a lot of territory—from the deepest seas of emotion to the airy spheres of the mind.

At your worst, the pair of you can cook up some very strange schemes. You can be devious, plotting, or escapist with each other. You can go to great lengths to get away from each other, then go through equally elaborate efforts to get back together. Yours can be a conflict between the need for constancy and restless promiscuity.

At best, you are the perfect blend of prolific creativity and mental dexterity. You can experiment in the emotions or in the mind, joining the power to penetrate deeply and the capacity to skim the surface. Of all the combinations in the Zodiac, yours will need the greatest latitude if it is to survive. You are curious about each other, yet remain in a way strangers. Your approach to life is different. Your minds work differently. Your aims are far apart. But these differences will fascinate you with each other and, strangely enough, will show you how similar you are.

Hints for Your Gemini Mate

In this union you learn very, very slowly that your Gemini mate is as enigmatic as you are deep. He or she says things unabashed that you have feared to think. Don't get mad when your mate lets the cat out of the bag socially or with your colleagues. Praise him or her, and wait to hear what other pearls of wisdom Gemini will confide to you in private. Gemini knows a lot of things, but can't always pull them together to make an organized whole. Be a tolerant listener, fair judge, and then go ahead and nudge your mate to perform. What you come up with together can last you both a lifetime. You don't have to be afraid your criticism will wither your Gemini partner; on the contrary, it acts as a catalyst. And don't be afraid to show your possessiveness; Gemini likes someone waiting in the wings. Also, ignore your mate's flirtations; they are superficial, friendly gestures.

SCORPIO—CANCER

Feeling rules your relationship. If it's a love affair you're having, it is rich both in powerful animal desires and in your souls' need to share a spiritual union. You're an emotional pair, the feelings running from the simplest everyday moods to deep, unconscious compulsions. Sexually, you may be drawn to each other with a hunger and passion that cannot be satisfied. You are both moody jealous types, private people whose territorial instincts resent any unwanted intruder who's stalking around. You are possessive, loyal, and obsessively protective of each other, a blend of sympathy and stamina, instinct and shrewd calculation.

At worst, you fight an emotional war—living under the shadow of jealousy, revenge, and insecurity. Materialism and greed can render you cynical and alienated, narrow, clannish, and power-oriented, unwilling to open up and unable to warm up or trust.

At best, you are the defenders of life. You have a natural instinct to mate and raise children, to maintain your religious and ethical codes, and to carry on the traditions of your ancestors with dignity and integrity. Love is the overpowering ingredient that floods your being and unites your combined spirits in fertility and fruitfulness. Share these.

Hints for Your Cancer Mate

Acquisitiveness runs through this relationship, complicated by your desire to show off what you have and what you know to your Cancer mate. Those tactics might have won your lover's heart in the courtship days, but you'll earn no admiration from them in the settling period. Cancer is a healer, not a competitor or warrior. Drawn initially to your magnetism and willpower, Cancer really loves you for the frail underside of your emotions—and expects to help you reassert yourself in crisis so both of you get the benefit of your so-called regenerative powers. Cancer basically is tougher than you, a fact you'll have to respect around the threshold of home, the corridors of career, the swinging doors of society. Don't let childish greed or jealousy destroy the finest alliance you can make. Let your sexual, emotional compatibility reassure you, then follow Cancer's instincts about money and things.

SCORPIO—LEO

You connect on deep emotional levels and can understand each other well, although you will not always agree. You are both aware of passion and desire. You both manage well in crisis situations and know how to emerge victorious from battle. You are connected by feeling, look up to one another, and find comfort and security in each other.

Sexually this is a steamy match, a hot-blooded battle of drives and feelings. Though drawn to it, you cannot stand domination from each other, and your conflict may be as fierce as your passions are. At worst, you are battling for control and manipulation. Jealousy, revenge, insecurity, and pain could take hold under the wrong influences. There could be a tapping of strength, a ruthless power struggle that would be difficult to end once it had begun.

At best, this is a tender, loving match, filled with consideration and concern. You help each other through crisis, feed each other, nourish each other sexually or emotionally, and enrich each other's spirit through the benefits of your individual experiences. You are as primitive and powerful as love and death, and your blend can imbue you both with the spirit of life. As tender as the reunion between parent and child, yours is a strong union, resistant to change or invasion and gifted with the power of regeneration.

Hints for Your Leo Mate

The lustiest emotions—a will to live and a sense of survival—got you and your Leo mate together in the first place, so don't douse cold water on the relationship at the first sign of pulling apart. Your tempos are different. Respect the often flickering, dulling, hidden quality of the Leo flame. Besides, your own Scorpio currents don't always run so straight and strong. And don't panic when one of Leo's pet projects blazes like a bonfire, attracting strangers, would-be lovers, hangers-on. Leo needs the flattery; allow it. The blaze is short-lived, but if in a fury of jealousy you tamper with the fuel or the spectators, you could cause your Leo partner to think twice about your loyalty. Never dampen the Leo flame with strategies, crises, ultimatums. Allow the heat of your Leo lover to carry you smoothly onward and upward.

SCORPIO—VIRGO

You're both quick-witted and clever, the possessors of shining intellect. When you get on a subject you both love, you're a pair of eager bloodhounds, covering every square inch of a topic. You've both got sharp tongues and caustic wit. The combat between you can be deadly, for you both know how to wound the other person. You can both be possessive and manipulative, compulsive and uptight. But you can also come through for each other and save the day with advice, criticism, encouragement, and supportive trust.

Work and sex will be important to your relationship as long as you know each other. Conflicts will arise between passionate desire and emotional coldness, between wanting too much and not wanting enough. But you are generally harmonious, despite your competitiveness, fretting, and moods. Your mental and sexual union can be deep and meaningful though your contacts may be few and far between rather than constant.

Because of your association, your friendships and even your life objectives may change permanently. Your relationship can be a conspiratorial one like that of a dangerous extremist and his accomplice. You are a blend of intensity and coolness. At best your relationship resembles that of pals or cousins, sharing a powerful kinship nothing can destroy. Criticism and incisive observation are your mutual assets. Your union can reflect the marriage of artistry and artisanship, creativity and practicality.

Hints for Your Virgo Mate

This relationship works best when you treat your Virgo mate as the intellectual colleague that she or he is. Both of you are healers; your combined talents will make everything right with the world, or at least that's the way you two are supposed to see things. Both of you are fixers; enjoy splitting the tasks of identifying a problem, analyzing the problem, solving the problem. Allow even your lovemaking to be subjected to the scrutiny and analysis that Virgo dearly loves. If your mate ever tries to pretend that he or she isn't really turned on, just get sexier; don't act like you're being rejected. Sometimes the littlest things give Virgo a chill, but a rigidly icy partner is not what you want; that could happen, though, if criticism comes from you. Also avoid heavy emotional scenes from which your partner will recoil. Keeping you together is at least one project in common.

SCORPIO—LIBRA

Because of you, Libra will learn how to survive financially. Contact with you will either awaken Libra's greed or kill it. A whole new sense of values will develop over time in your Libra partner. Your ideas of control and strength affect profoundly the Libra sense of yielding to the other person.

You are drawn to Libra, but the fear of surrendering your ego will send you fleeing time and again. It is hard for you not to trust wholly, but Libra's uncertainty is often your undoing. As Libra grows in strength and self-knowledge, your decisiveness is challenged.

In a relationship with Libra, you can feel trapped or drawn irresistibly into it. Your life slowly changes, because the relationship can bring a permanent revision of everything you hold dear. So powerful is the attraction that you cannot ever imagine being separated. You may believe you are naturally connected forever.

Libra is the source of life-giving inspiration and spiritual power. For Scorpio this is the most complex relationship possible. Through this relationship you will deal with trust, forgiveness, disillusion, sacrifice, cosmic obedience, and inner regeneration.

Hints for Your Libra Mate

Try always to keep the romanticism of your courtship alive with your Libra mate. Arrange your social lives so that Libra can see you surrendering to his or her graceful charms, gay party manner, unbelievably good-looking costuming. A honeymoon quality persisting in this relationship will make it work splendidly. Don't get to nit-picking about details, decisions; never force Libra into making a decision alone. With you brooding about the future and with Libra wondering how to avoid worrying about the future, the relationship could get bogged down in false starts and stops. If you brood less, Libra will wonder less, and both of you will be able to get on with the business of everyday living. Save the weekends for the bright glitter and chatter of company that make both of you know you're the loveliest couple in town.

SCORPIO—SCORPIO

Once you two have united, you will never again be truly free. Your involvement is profoundly deep, lasting, and emotional. You both live on the horizon between light and dark, life and death. You are both capable of vengeance and jealousy, greed and lust. You have enormous cunning, and like to control your opponent from a position of utter strength.

Strangely enough, you don't often come to a fight-to-the-death struggle. You both prefer the indirect approach. More importantly, you have a certain respect and understanding for each other that lends mutual support in your conscious striving to develop your creative potentials and transform yourselves into higher beings. No matter how emotionally involved you get, you can regain control of yourselves when you need to, and bring the issues back to cold, hard business.

Your attraction to each other is compulsive, and you are joined by your extreme tastes, ambitions, and desires. You both need privacy, but without saying much you can communicate with each other on a level where most other people would be forbidden entrance. Your interest in sex is total and mutual. When you make peace and love each other, it's forever. Although your rivalries never die, you are loyal and protective, giving each other the power to be reborn through keen perception and strong love.

Hints for Your Scorpio Mate

It's amazing what you two Scorpio lovers allow with each other: experimentation, polygamy, distance, space. Any of those stances with any other mate in the Zodiac would not be labeled in such nonjudgmental terms, and would warrant venemous attack, punishing possessiveness. Now how can you keep it that way? Think about your own goals of regeneration; apply them with your Scorpio mate. You want the freedom to feel, heal, renew, recreate. Your mate should have it, too. But the decision must come from shared discussions, shared goals. If your mate is more determined than you are to live life a certain way, without your input, try to sustain the independence that gives you. If your mate is not as determined as you are, use your power to make separateness and freedom worthwhile goals—free-flowing currents joyously joining together as need and mood suit you both.

SCORPIO—SAGITTARIUS

Your passion for enjoyment draws you to Sagittarius, lifts you out of the depths, broadens your experience, and provides new opportunities for improving the character of your life. Sagittarius loves you with a compulsion that is often so confusing and overpowering that you could be the undoing of your Sagittarius mate. Although you could pose baffling questions that might exist as long as your relationship lasts, you can also be instrumental in awakening spirituality, deeper awareness, and higher consciousness in your partner.

You can deceive yourselves by fostering false hopes in each other, and together you can be a selfish pair of irresponsible children. On the other hand, you both share a healthy stamina and resilience to life's situations. You can save each other from brooding about impossibilities, for you both love pleasure, luxuries, and the joys of living. You share a taste for adventure and a desire to do something exciting, big, spectacular. You can brighten each other's horizons, raise each other's consciousness, share your intensity, and enlarge your scope.

Sagittarius can change your values and be your greatest asset. Appreciate the opportunity and reciprocate by being emotionally generous. Strive for higher consciousness to achieve greater happiness.

Hints for Your Sagittarius Mate

In this relationship don't fall into the habit of asking your Sagittarius mate to be accountable—in thought, word, or deed. Sagittarius might never admonish you, but long before the gambit becomes a habit, Sagittarius will feel trapped and want to move on. But you can always solicit your mate's opinions, beliefs. In fact, the more you encourage Sagittarius to talk, the better able she or he will be to put into perspective some of those dreamy notions. Cherish your mate's idealism; you have a large dose of it yourself. You should also help your mate bridge the gap between big ideas and reality, even if it means taking charge and shepherding a project along. Your mate won't feel you're bossy or restricting here, because, after all, you are such splendid equals in lovemaking.

SCORPIO—CAPRICORN

As you develop a long-term relationship based on mutual respect you will be a source of strength to each other. Yours is a union of intensity and stability. Sexually this can be a powerful match, for your involvement is anything but light. You both share a need for strong ties, and the depth of your relationship will always show that. Games of power and control may be irresistible for you both, since the two of you are strong-willed cautious types who like to feel you are indispensable to your partner. You both need acceptance and want to be loved, honored, and obeyed. When you go to war, the war can last a long time. Neither of you is a total forgiver and forgetter, and you don't trust each other easily.

You are a no-nonsense combination of sexual magnetism and career drive, for you blend an otherworldly creativity with hardheaded ambition. Sometimes you are more successful apart than together. You are apt to be better friends than lovers.

Through loyalty and practical approaches to your problems, your relationship is sure to grow and deepen, no matter how long it takes. And it will take time, for you are both hard to know. You are both able, courageous people. No struggle is too great for you both to undertake. You both love to emerge unscathed from the problems of life, and the older you get the tougher you get. Maturity will be of great benefit to your association.

Hints for Your Capricorn Mate

No matter what your rank or privilege is relative to your Capricorn mate, you are undeniably the authority in the emotion department. Capricorn, unlike some zodiacal types, won't mind if you give intense instruction in this area. After all, you're turning Capricorn on, something that is hard for him or her to do on their own behalf. Yes, Capricorn needs an authority figure to sponsor an open, lusty sexuality. Here, too, you can be the grand master. Concentrate on these areas to develop your relationship to its fullest. You won't have much cause for brooding or discord in other areas. Capricorn, like you, has a strong will, a commitment to problem solving, and a huge desire to get on with life and get the most out of it. But if you need to play the subordinate somewhere, let Capricorn teach you how to make your creativity work for you.

SCORPIO—AQUARIUS

Diplomacy, compromise, and love of justice are key solutions to the dilemma of attachment and freedom that you two will face. Whatever conflicts arise between togetherness and separateness can shatter your dreams of peace. But facing the storms can bring you both to a new and exciting understanding of yourselves as individuals and in relation to each other. You are both looking for security with independence. Yet you both may find it hard to make total and long-lasting commitments. It is very difficult for you both to relax and let yourselves be free. Yet when you become possessive, you fear each other.

Your conflicts are between the intimate one-to-one relationships of your forebears and the free-style open scenes of experimentation. You struggle between a need for deep sexual involvements and a need for open nonsexual contacts with friends and fellow human beings in a spirit of community and harmony. Your relationship can vary from tenderness, intensity, nourishment, and growth to abrupt coldness, separation, and a peculiar lack of care and feeling.

You can have a long-lasting relationship provided you don't get too bossy and possessive and provided you don't leave your partner in the lurch to show your independence. Some rules are made to be broken. Mature individuals who love each other will have the respect and concern of their partners without demanding them. When your partner trusts you, you will have your security and freedom, too.

Hints for Your Aquarius Mate

You two can have a lot of fun talking about the brave new world while you're both heroically tending to the miserable tasks of this one. At the very least, you can document your Aquarius mate's suspicions that all is not well by delivering an ongoing, tragically personal account of the inequities and perils of life. And you are a sympathetic listener when Aquarius ingeniously describes a new design for living. Of course, all the while both of you are washing dishes, watering plants, changing the kitty litter, tripping back and forth to the laundry, sorting monthly bills. Aren't you? These little responsibilities are not very romantic, but they keep your house together and give you both time and space to dwell on the bigger issues and to mentally solve them. Let your Aquarius mate be your intellectual hero. For him or her, you are the victor in love and sex.

SCORPIO—PISCES

When you fall in love with Pisces, there is always romance, passion, confusion, indecision, disappointment, and a sweet but maddening intoxication. Together you can create a channel for mutual desires. And you both flow into a sea of emotion, swept away by love, sex, and mystery. Pisces responds to the masterful drive of Scorpio. Scorpio cuts through the Pisces indecision like a scalpel. Your purifying thrust acts like a strong conscience, healing and strengthening the Pisces mind.

Of all the combinations of zodiacal signs, yours has the most potential for effecting changes in each other's lives for good or ill. At worst you are obsessed and driven, plaguing yourselves and each other with a mixture of cruelty, self-indulgence, and escapism, addicted to pleasures and the drama of emotional conflict and personal pain, trapped in an endless cycle of attraction and repulsion.

The explosive energy you as a Scorpio feel is greatly different from the search your Pisces undertakes. Pisces is searching for self-knowledge through meditation, travel, learning, and education. Your paths may be different until you converge and meet at a point of no return.

At best, your relationship can take on mythic proportions. It can become a love affair with a sense of mission or greater purpose. Together you are the union of the selfless servant and the healer. You can break free from social rules, emotional limitations, and earthly obstacles. Together you can perform, create, enjoy, make love in an eternal union of the mind, body, and spirit.

Hints for Your Pisces Mates

Just because you both are water signs doesn't mean that you can safely inhabit the same niche without a lot of defensive maneuvering. Like the scorpion which is your symbol, you may lurk at water's edge to sting your Pisces partner as he or she glides by. And your partner, double fish like the Pisces symbol, may swim in two totally opposite directions to get away from you. The best adaptation for this relationship is for each of you to keep some parts of your lives separate and distinct. Make a contract disallowing complaints and criticism about the other's territory. Perhaps for the habitats you do share there should also be stringent rules about who does what when, such as household chores, entertaining, use of the computer, typewriter, telephone. You'll interact swimmingly, though, in the realms of sex and emotion.

SCORPIO:
YOUR PROGRESSED SUN

WHAT IS YOUR NEW SIGN

Your birth sign, or Sun sign, is the central core of your whole personality. It symbolizes everything you try to do and be. It is your main streak, your major source of power, vitality, and life. But as you live you learn, and as you learn you progress. The element in your horoscope that measures your progress is called the Progressed Sun. It is the symbol of your growth on Earth, and represents new threads that run through your life. The Progressed Sun measures big changes, turning points, and major decisions. It will often describe the path you are taking toward the fulfillment of your desires.

Below you will find brief descriptions of the Progressed Sun in three signs. According to the table on page 43, find out about your Progressed Sun and see how and where you fit into the cosmic scheme. Each period lasts about 30 years, so watch and see how dramatic these changes turn out to be.

If Your Sun Is Progressing Into—

SAGITTARIUS, look up, for your life will be much brighter from now on. You will find great encouragement for living, for sports, for travel. Your power of learning will increase. Religion, politics, philosophy, and higher learning will enter your life at this time.

Though your aims may be unrealistic and over-expansive, you will be buoyed up by good cheer.

CAPRICORN, you will grow more serious during this period. Plans that are unrealistic will come to no good end. You will need to add structure to your life, confront your limitations, and examine the boundaries that govern your particular life circumstances. You'll have to start working harder to get what you want. Success will be yours during this period as long as you climb toward it.

AQUARIUS, you'll be wanting freedom from the restrictions of the past years. You will want to break new territory, throw off limitations, start fresh, and experiment with new things and new people. You will have contact with groups, societies, and friends. It is a time for advancements as you put past reversals behind you and into perspective.

HOW TO USE THE TABLE

Look for your birthday in the table on the facing page. Then under the appropriate column, find out approximately when your Progressed Sun will lead you to a new sign. From that point on, for 30 years, the thread of your life will run through that sign. Read the definitions on the preceding pages and see exactly how that life thread will develop.

For example, if your birthday is October 30, your Progressed Sun will enter Sagittarius around your 24th birthday and will travel through Sagittarius until you are 54 years old. Your Progressed Sun will then move into Capricorn. Reading the definitions of Sagittarius and Capricorn will tell you much about your major involvements and interests during those years.

YOUR PROGRESSED SUN

If your birthday falls on:	start looking at SAGITTARIUS at age	start looking at CAPRICORN at age	start looking at AQUARIUS at age
Oct. 23–24	30	60	90
25	29	59	89
26	28	58	88
27	27	57	87
28	26	56	86
29	25	55	85
30	24	54	84
31	23	53	83
November 1	22	52	82
2	21	51	81
3	20	50	80
4	19	49	79
5	18	48	78
6	17	47	77
7	16	46	76
8	15	45	75
9	14	44	74
10	13	43	73
11	12	42	72
12	11	41	71
13	10	40	70
14	9	39	69
15	8	38	68
16	7	37	67
17	6	36	66
18	5	35	65
19	4	34	64
20	3	33	63
21	2	32	62
22	1	31	61

SCORPIO BIRTHDAYS

Oct. 23	Sarah Bernhardt, Johnny Carson
Oct. 24	Moss Hart, Jimmy Dawkins
Oct. 25	Pablo Picasso, Helen Reddy
Oct. 26	Mahalia Jackson, Margaret Leighton
Oct. 27	Teddy Roosevelt, Ruby Dee, Sylvia Plath
Oct. 28	Elsa Lancaster, Jonas Salk
Oct. 29	Fanny Brice, Bill Mauldin
Oct. 30	Charles Atlas, Grace Slick
Oct. 31	Dale Evans, Ethel Waters
Nov. 1	Stephen Crane, Victoria de Los Angelos
Nov. 2	Daniel Boone, Burt Lancaster
Nov. 3	Andre Malraux
Nov. 4	Will Rogers, Walter Cronkite
Nov. 5	Roy Rogers, Art Garfunkel
Nov. 6	James Jones, Mike Nichols
Nov. 7	Marie Curie, Joni Mitchell
Nov. 8	Katharine Hepburn, Margaret Mitchell
Nov. 9	Hedy Lamarr, Marie Dressler
Nov. 10	Martin Luther, Richard Burton
Nov. 11	Abigal Adams, Kurt Vonnegut
Nov. 12	Grace Kelly, Elizabeth Stanton
Nov. 13	Robert Louis Stevenson, Eugene Ionesco
Nov. 14	Jawaharlal Nehru, Marya Mannes
Nov. 15	Marianne Moore, Georgia O'Keefe
Nov. 16	Burgess Meredith
Nov. 17	Rock Hudson
Nov. 18	Eugene Ormandy, Dorothy Dix
Nov. 19	Indira Gandhi, Dick Cavett
Nov. 20	Bobby Kennedy, Estelle Parsons
Nov. 21	Voltaire, Goldie Hawn, Marlo Thomas
Nov. 22	George Eliot, Geraldine Page, Billie Jean King

CAN ASTROLOGY PREDICT THE FUTURE?

Can astrology really peer into the future? By studying the planets and the stars is it possible to look years ahead and make predictions for our lives? How can we draw the line between ignorant superstition and cosmic mystery? We live in a very civilized world, to be sure. We consider ourselves modern, enlightened individuals. Yet few of us can resist the temptation to take a peek at the future when we think it's possible. Why? What is the basis of such universal curiosity?

The answer is simple. Astrology works, and you don't have to be a magician to find that out. We certainly can't prove astrology simply by taking a look at the astonishing number of people who believe in it, but such figures do make us wonder what lies behind such widespread popularity. Everywhere in the world hundreds of thousands of serious, intelligent people are charting, studying, and interpreting the positions of the planets and stars every day. Every facet of the media dispenses daily astrological bulletins to millions of curious seekers. In Eastern countries, the source of many wisdoms handed down to us from antiquity, astrology still has a vital place. Why? Surrounded as we are by sophisticated scientific method, how does astrology, with all its bizarre symbolism and mysterious meaning, survive so magnificently? The answer remains the same. It works.

Nobody knows exactly where astrological knowledge came from. We have references to it dating back to the dawn of human history. Wherever there was a stirring of human consciousness, people began to observe the natural cycles and rhythms that sustained their life. The diversity of human behavior must have been evident even to the first students of consciousness. Yet the basic similarity between members of the human family must have led to the search for some common source, some greater point of origin somehow linked to the heavenly bodies ruling our sense of life and time. The ancient world of Mesopotamia, Chaldea, and Egypt was a highly developed center of astronomical observation and astrological interpretation of heavenly phenomena and their resultant effects on human life.

Amid the seeming chaos of a mysterious unknown universe, people from earliest times sought to classify, define, and organize the world around them. Order: that's what the human mind has always striven to maintain in an unceasing battle with its natural counterpart, chaos, or entropy. We build cities, countries, and empires, subjugating nature to a point of near defeat, and then . . . civilization collapses, empires fall, and cities crumble. Nature reclaims the wilderness. Shelly's poem *Ozymandias* is a hymn to the battle between order and chaos. The narrator tells us about a statue, broken, shattered, and half-sunk somewhere in the middle of a distant desert. The inscription reads: "Look on my works, ye mighty, and despair." And then we are told: "Nothing beside remains. Round the decay of that colossal wreck, boundless and bare, the lone and level sands stretch far away."

People always feared the entropy that seemed to lurk in nature. So we found permanence and constancy in the regular movements of the Sun, Moon, and planets and in the positions of the stars. Traditions sprang up from observations of the seasons and crops. Relationships were noted between phenomena in nature and the configurations of the heavenly bodies. This "synchronicity," as it was later called by Carl Jung, extended to thought, mood, and behavior, and as such developed the astrological archetypes handed down to us today.

Astrology, a regal science of the stars in the old days, was made available to the king, who was informed of impending events in the heavens, translated of course to their earthly meanings by trusted astrologers. True, astrological knowledge in its infant stages was rudimentary and beset with many superstitions and false premises. But those same dangers exist today in any investigation of occult or mystical subjects. In the East, reverence for astrology is part of religion. Astrologer-astronomers have held respected positions in government and have taken part in advisory councils on many momentous issues. The duties of the court astrologer, whose office was one of the most important in the land, were clearly defined, as early records show.

Here in our sleek Western world, astrology glimmers on, perhaps more brilliantly than ever. With all of our technological wonders and complex urbanized environments, we look to astrology even now to cut through artificiality, dehumanization, and all the materialism of contemporary life, while we gather precious information that helps us live in that material world. Astrology helps us restore balance and get in step with our own rhythms and the rhythms of nature.

Intelligent investigation of astrology (or the practical application of it) need not mean blind acceptance. We only need to see it working, see our own lives confirming its principles every day, in order to accept and understand it more. To understand ourselves is to know ourselves and to know all. This book can help you to do that—to understand yourself and through understanding develop your own resources and potentials as a rich human being.

YOUR PLACE AMONG THE STARS

Humanity finds itself at the center of a vast personal universe that extends infinitely outward in all directions. In that sense each is a kind of star radiating, as our Sun does, to all bodies everywhere. These vibrations, whether loving, helpful, or destructive, extend outward and generate a kind of "atmosphere" in which woman and man move. The way we relate to everything around us—our joy or our sorrow—becomes a living part of us. Our loved ones and our enemies become the objects of our projected radiations, for better or worse. Our bodies and faces reflect thoughts and emotions much the way light from the Sun reflects the massive reactions occurring deep within its interior. This energy and light reach all who enter its sphere of influence.

Our own personal radiations are just as potent in their own way, really. The reactions that go on deep within us profoundly affect our way of thinking and acting. Our feelings of joy or satisfaction, frustration or anger, must eventually find an outlet. Otherwise we experience the psychological or physiological repercussions of repression. If we can't have a good cry, tell someone our troubles, or express love, we soon feel very bad indeed.

As far as our physical selves are concerned, there is a direct relationship between our outer lives, inner reactions and actions, and the effects on our physical body. We all know the feeling of being startled by the sudden ring of a telephone, or the simple frustration of missing a bus. In fact, our minds and bodies are constantly reacting to outside forces. At the same time we, too, are generating actions that will cause a reaction in someone else. You may suddenly decide to phone a friend. If you are a bus driver you might speed along on your way and leave behind an angry would-be passenger. Whatever the case, mind and body are in close communication and they both reflect each other's condition. Next time you're really angry take a good long look in the mirror!

In terms of human evolution, our ability to understand, control, and ultimately change ourselves will naturally affect all of our outside relationships. Astrology is invaluable to helping us comprehend our inner selves. It is a useful tool in helping us retain our integrity, while cooperating with and living in a world full of other human beings.

Let's go back to our original question: Can astrology predict the future? To know that, we must come to an understanding of what the future is.

In simplest terms the future is the natural next step to the present, just as the present is a natural progression from the past. Although our minds can move from one to the other, there is a thread of continuity between past, present, and future that joins them together in a coherent sequence. If you are reading this book at this moment, it is the result of a real conscious choice you made in the recent past. That is, you chose to find out what was on these pages, picked up the book, and opened it. Because of this choice you may know yourself better in the future. It's as simple as that.

Knowing ourselves is the key to being able to predict and understand our own future. To learn from past experiences, choices, and actions is to fully grasp the present. Coming to grips with the present is to be master of the future.

"Know thyself" is a motto that takes us back to the philosophers of ancient Greece. Mystery religions and cults of initiation throughout the ancient world, schools of mystical discipline, yoga and mental expansion have always been guardians of this one sacred phrase. Know thyself. Of course, that's easy to say. But how do you go about it when there are so many conflicts in our lives and different parts of our personalities? How do we know when we are really "being ourselves" and not merely being influenced by the things we read or see on television, or by the people around us? How can we differentiate the various parts of our character and still remain whole?

There are many methods of classifying human beings into types. Body shapes, muscular types, blood types, and genetic types are only a few. Psychology has its own ways of classifying human beings according to their behavior. Anthropology studies human evolution as the body-mind response to environment. Biology watches physical development and adaptations in body structure. These fields provide valuable information about human beings and the ways they survive, grow, and change in their search for their place in eternity. Yet these branches of science have been separate and fragmented. Their contribution has been to provide theories and data, yes, but no lasting solutions to the human problems that have existed since the first two creatures realized they had two separate identities.

It's often difficult to classify yourself according to these different schemes. It's not easy to be objective about yourself. Some things are hard to face; others are hard to see. The different perspectives afforded to us by studying the human organism from all these different disciplines may seem contradictory when they are all really trying to integrate humankind into the whole of the cosmic scheme.

Astrology can help these disciplines unite to seek a broader and deeper approach to universal human issues. Astrology's point of view is vast. It transcends racial, ethnic, genetic, environmental, and even historical criteria, yet somehow includes them all. Astrology embraces the totality of human experience, then sets about to examine the relationships that are created within that experience.

We don't simply say, "The planets cause this or that." Rather than merely isolating cause or effect, astrology has unified the ideas of cause and effect. Concepts of past, present, and future merge and become, as we shall see a little later on, like stepping-stones across the great stream of mind. Observations of people and the environment have developed the astrological principles of planetary "influence," but it must be remembered that if there is actual influence, it is mutual. As the planets influence us, so we influence them, for we are forever joined to all past and future motion of the heavenly bodies. This is the foundation of astrology as it has been built up over the centuries.

ORDER VS. CHAOS

But is it all written in the stars? Is it destined that empires should thrive and flourish, kings reign, lovers love, and then . . . decay, ruin, and natural disintegration hold sway? Have we anything to do with determining the cycles of order and chaos? The art of the true astrologer depends on his ability to uncover new information, place it upon the grid of data already collected, and then interpret what he sees as accurate probability in human existence. There may be a paradox here. If we can predict that birds will fly south, could we not, with enough time and samples for observation, determine their ultimate fate when they arrive in the south?

The paradox is that there is no paradox at all. Order and chaos exist together simultaneously in one observable universe. At some remote point in time and space the Earth was formed, and for one reason or another, life appeared here. Whether the appearance of life on planets is a usual phenomenon or an unrepeated accident we can only speculate at this moment. But our Earth and all living things upon its surface conform to certain laws of physical materiality that our observations have led us to write down and contemplate. All creatures, from the one-celled ameba to a man hurrying home at rush hour, have some basic traits in common. Life in its organization goes from the simple to the complex with a perfection and order that is both awesome and inspiring. If there were no order to our physical world, an apple could turn into a worm and cows could be butterflies.

But the world is an integrated whole, unified with every other part of creation. When nature does take an unexpected turn, we call that a mutation. This is the exciting card in the program of living experience that tells us not everything is written at all. Spontaneity is real. Change is real. Freedom from the expected norm is real. We have seen in nature that only those mutations that can adapt to changes in their environment and continue reproducing themselves will survive. But possibilities are open for sudden transformation, and that keeps the whole world growing.

FREE CHOICE AND
THE VALUE OF PREDICTIONS

Now it's time to turn our attention to the matter of predictions. That was our original question after all: Can astrology peer into the future? Well, astrological prognostication is an awe-inspiring art and requires deep philosophical consideration before it is to be undertaken. Not only are there many grids that must be laid one upon the other before such predictions can be made, but there are ethical issues that plague every student of the stars. How much can you really see? How much should you tell? What is the difference between revealing valuable data and disclosing negative or harmful programing?

If an astrologer tells you only the good things, you'll have little confidence in the analysis when you are passing through crisis. On the other hand, if the astrologer is a prophet of doom who can see nothing but the dark clouds on the horizon, you will eventually have to reject astrology because you will come to associate it with the bad luck in your life.

Astrology itself is beyond any practitioner's capacity to grasp it all. Unrealistic utopianism or gloomy determinism reflect not the truth of astrology but the truth of the astrologer interpreting what he sees. In order to solve problems and make accurate predictions, you have to be *able* to look on the dark side of things without dwelling there. You have to be able to take a look at all the possibilities, all the possible meanings of a certain planetary influence without jumping to premature conclusions. Objective scanning and assessment take much practice and great skill.

No matter how skilled the astrologer is, he cannot assume the responsibility for your life. Only you can take that responsibility as your life unfolds. In a way, the predictions of this book are glancing ahead up the road, much the way a road map can indicate turns up ahead this way or that. You, however, are still driving the car.

What, then, is a horoscope? If it is a picture of you at your moment of birth, are you then frozen forever in time and space, unable to budge or deviate from the harsh, unyielding declarations of the stars? Not at all.

The universe is always in motion. Each moment follows the moment before it. As the present is the result of all past choices and action, so the future is the result of today's choices. But if we can go to a planetary calendar and see where planets will be located two years from now, then how can individual free choice exist? This is a question that has haunted authors and philosophers since the first thinkers recorded their thoughts. In the end, of course, we must all reason things out for ourselves and come to our own conclusions. It is easy to be impressed or influenced by people who seem to know a lot more than we do, but in reality we must all find codes of beliefs with which we are the most comfortable.

But if we can stretch our imaginations up, up above the line of time as it exists from one point to another, we can almost see past, present, and future, all together. We can almost feel this vibrant thread of creative free choice that pushes forward at every moment, actually causing the future to happen! Free will, that force that changes the entire course of a stream, exists within the stream of mind itself—the collective mind, or intelligence, of humanity. Past, present, and future are mere stepping-stones across that great current.

Our lives continue a thread of an intelligent mind

that existed before we were born and will exist after we die. It is like an endless relay race. At birth we pick up a torch and carry it, lighting the way with that miraculous light of consciousness of immortality. Then we pass it on to others when we die. What we call the *unconscious* may be part of this great stream of mind, which learns and shares experiences with everything that has ever lived or will ever live on this world or any other.

Yet we all come to Earth with different family circumstances, backgrounds, and characteristics. We all come to life with different planetary configurations. Indeed each person *is* different, yet we are all the same. We have different tasks or responsibilities or lifestyles, but underneath we share a common current—the powerful stream of human intelligence. Each of us has different sets of circumstances to deal with because of the choices he or she has made in the past. We all possess different assets and have different resources to fall back on, weaknesses to strengthen, and sides of our nature to transform. We are all what we are now because of what we were before. The present is the sum of the past. And we will be what we will be in the future because of what we are now.

It is foolish to pretend that there are no specific boundaries or limitations to any of our particular lives. Family background, racial, cultural, or religious indoctrinations, physical characteristics, these are all inescapable facts of our being that must be incorporated and accepted into our maturing mind. But each person possesses the capacity for breakthrough, forgiveness, and total transformation. It has taken millions of years since people first began to walk upright. We cannot expect an overnight evolution to take place. There are many things about our personalities that are very much like our parents. Sometimes that thought makes us uncomfortable, but it's true.

It's also true that we are not our parents. You are

you, just you, and nobody else but you. That's one of the wondrous aspects of astrology. The levels on which each planetary configuration works out will vary from individual to individual. Often an aspect of selfishness will be manifested in one person, yet in another it may appear as sacrifice and kindness.

Development is inevitable in human consciousness. But the direction of that development is not. As plants will bend toward the light as they grow, so there is the possibility for the human mind to grow toward the light of integrity and truth. The Age of Aquarius that everyone is talking about must first take place within each human's mind and heart. An era of peace, freedom, and community cannot be legislated by any government, no matter how liberal. It has to be a spontaneous flow of human spirit and fellowship. It will be a magnificent dawning on the globe of consciousness that reflects the joy of the human heart to be part of the great stream of intelligence and love. It must be generated by an enlightened, realistic humanity. There's no law that can put it into effect, no magic potion to drink that will make it all come true. It will be the result of all people's efforts to assume their personal and social responsibilities and to carve out a new destiny for humankind.

As you read the predictions in this book, bear in mind that they have been calculated by means of planetary positions for whole groups of people. Thus their value lies in your ability to coordinate what you read with the nature of your life's circumstances at the present time. You have seen how many complex relationships must be analyzed in individual horoscopes before sensible accurate conclusions can be drawn. No matter what the indications, a person has his or her own life, own intelligence, basic native strength that must ultimately be the source of action and purpose. When you are living truthfully and in harmony with what you know is right, there are no forces, threats, or obstacles that can defeat you.

With these predictions, read the overall pattern and see how rhythms begin to emerge. They are not caused by remote alien forces, millions of miles out in space. You and the planets are one. What you do, they do. What they do, you do. But can you change their course? No, but you cannot change many of your basic characteristics either. Still, within that already existing framework, you are the master. You can still differentiate between what is right for you and what is not. You can seize opportunities and act on them, you can create beauty and seek love.

The purpose of looking ahead is not to scare yourself. Look ahead to enlarge your perspective, enhance your overall view of the life *you* are developing. Difficult periods cause stress certainly, but at the same time they give you the chance to reassess your condition, restate and redefine exactly what is important to you, so you can cherish your life more. Joyous periods should be lived to the fullest with the happiness and exuberance that each person richly deserves.

YOUR HOROSCOPE AND THE ZODIAC

It's possible that in your own body, as you read this passage, there exist atoms as old as time itself. You could well be the proud possessor of some carbon and hydrogen (two necessary elements in the development of life) that came into being in the heart of a star billions and billions of years ago. That star could have exploded and cast its matter far into space. This matter could have formed another star, and then another, until finally our Sun was born. From the Sun's nuclear reactions came the material that later formed the planets—and maybe some of that primeval carbon or hydrogen. That material could have become part of the Earth, part of an early ocean, even early life. These same atoms could well have been carried down to the present day, to this very moment as you read this book. It's really quite possible. You can see how everything is linked to everything else. Our Earth now exists in a gigantic universe that showers it constantly with rays and invisible particles. You are the point into which all these energies and influences have been focused. You are the prism through which all the light of outer space is being refracted. You are literally a reflection of all the planets and stars.

Your horoscope is a picture of the sky at the moment of your birth. It's like a gigantic snapshot of the positions of the planets and stars, taken from Earth. Of course, the planets never stop moving around the Sun even for the briefest moment, and you represent that motion as it was occurring at the exact hour of your birth at the precise location on the Earth where you were born.

When an astrologer is going to read your chart, he or she asks you for the month, day, and year of your birth. She also needs the exact time and place. With this information he sets about consulting various charts and tables in his calculation of the specific positions of the Sun, Moon, and stars, relative to your birthplace when you came to Earth. Then he or she locates them by means of the *Zodiac*.

The Zodiac is a group of stars, centered against the Sun's apparent path around the Earth, and these star groups are divided into twelve equal segments, or *signs*. What we are actually dividing up is the Earth's path around the Sun. But from our point of view here on Earth, it seems as if the Sun is making a great circle around our planet in the sky, so we say it's the Sun's apparent path. This twelvefold division, the Zodiac, is like a mammoth address system for any body in the sky. At any given moment, the planets can all be located at a specific point along this path.

Now where are you in this system? First you look to your *Sun sign*—the section of the Zodiac that the Sun occupied when you were born. A great part of your character, in fact the central thread of your whole being, is described by your Sun sign. Each sign of the Zodiac has certain basic traits associated with it. Since the Sun remains in each sign for about thirty days, that divides the population into twelve major character types. Of course, not everybody born the same month will have the same character, but you'll be amazed at how many fundamental traits you share with your astrological cousins of the same birth sign, no matter how many environmental differences you boast.

The dates on which the Sun sign changes will vary from year to year. That is why some people born near the *cusp*, or edge, of a sign have difficulty determining their true birth sign without the aid of an astrologer who can plot precisely the Sun's apparent motion (the Earth's motion) for any given year. But to help you find your true Sun sign, a Table of Cusp Dates for the years 1900 to 2000 is provided for you on page 17.

Here are the twelve signs of the Zodiac as western astrology has recorded them. Listed also are the symbols associated with them and the *approximate* dates when the Sun enters and exits each sign for the year 1998.

Aries	Ram	March 20–April 20
Taurus	Bull	April 20–May 21
Gemini	Twins	May 21–June 21
Cancer	Crab	June 21–July 22
Leo	Lion	July 22–August 23
Virgo	Virgin	August 23–September 23
Libra	Scales	September 23–October 23
Scorpio	Scorpion	October 23–November 22
Sagittarius	Archer	November 22–December 21
Capricorn	Sea Goat	December 21–January 20
Aquarius	Water Bearer	January 20–February 18
Pisces	Fish	February 18-March 20

In a horoscope the *Rising sign*, or Ascendant, is often considered to be as important as the Sun sign. In a later chapter (see pages 82–84) the Rising sign is discussed in detail. But to help you determine your own Rising sign, a Table of Rising Signs is provided for you on pages 20–21.

THE SIGNS OF THE ZODIAC

The signs of the Zodiac are an ingenious and complex summary of human behavioral and physical types, handed down from generation to generation through the bodies of all people in their hereditary material and through their minds. On the following pages you will find brief descriptions of all twelve signs in their highest and most ideal expression.

ARIES
The Sign of the Ram

Aries is the first sign of the Zodiac, and marks the beginning of springtime and the birth of the year. In spring the Earth begins its ascent upward and tips its North Pole toward the Sun. During this time the life-giving force of the Sun streams toward Earth, bathing our planet with the kiss of warmth and life. Plants start growing. Life wakes up. No more waiting. No more patience. The message has come from the Sun: Time to live!

Aries is the sign of the Self and is the crusade for the right of an individual to live in unimpeachable freedom. It represents the supremacy of the human will over all obstacles, limitations, and threats. In Aries there is unlimited energy, optimism, and daring, for it is the pioneer in search of a new world. It is the story of success and renewal, championship, and victory. It is the living spirit of resilience and the power to be yourself, free from all restrictions and conditioning. There is no pattern you *have* to repeat, nobody's rule you *have* to follow.

Confidence and positive action are born in Aries, with little thought or fear of the past. Life is as magic as sunrise, with all the creative potential ahead of you for a new day. Activity, energy, and adventure characterize this sign. In this sector of the Zodiac there is amazing strength, forthrightness, honesty, and a stubborn refusal to accept defeat. The Aries nature is forgiving, persuasive, masterful, and decisive.

In short, Aries is the magic spark of life and being, the source of all initiative, courage, independence, and self-esteem.

TAURUS
The Sign of the Bull

Taurus is wealth. It is not just money, property, and the richness of material possessions, but also a wealth of the spirit. Taurus rules everything in the visible world we see, touch, hear, smell, taste—the Earth, sea, and sky—everything we normally consider "real." It is the sign of economy and reserve, for it is a mixture of thrift and luxury, generosity and practicality. It is a blend of the spiritual and material, for the fertility of the sign is unlimited, and in this sense it is the mystical bank of life. Yet it must hold the fruit of its efforts in its hands and seeks to realize its fantasy-rich imagination with tangible rewards.

Loyalty and endurance make this sign perhaps the most stable of all. We can lean on Taurus, count on it,

and it makes our earthly lives comfortable, safe, pleasurable. It is warm, sensitive, loving, and capable of
magnificent, joyful sensations. It is conservative and
pragmatic, with a need to be sure of each step forward.
It is the capacity to plan around eventualities without
living in the future. Steadfast and constant, this is a
sturdy combination of ruggedness and beauty, gentle-
ness and unshakability of purpose. It is the point at
which we join body and soul. Unselfish friend and loyal
companion, Taurus is profoundly noble and openly humanitarian. Tenacity and concentration slow the energy down to bring certain long-lasting rewards.

Taurus is a fertile resource and rich ground to grow in,
and we all need it for our ideas and plans to flourish. It is
the uncut diamond, symbolizing rich, raw tastes and a
deep need for satisfaction, refinement, and completion.

GEMINI
The Sign of the Twins

Gemini is the sign of mental brilliance. Communication
is developed to a high degree of fluidity, rapidity, fluency.
It is the chance for expressing ideas and relaying information from one place to another. Charming, debonair,
and lighthearted, it is a symbol of universal interest and
eternal curiosity. The mind is quick and advanced, with a
lightning-like ability to assimilate data.

It is the successful manipulation of verbal or visual
language and the capacity to meet all events with ob-
jectivity and intelligence. It is light, quick wit, with a
comic satiric twist. Gemini is the sign of writing or
speaking.

Gemini is the willingness to try anything once, a need to wander and explore, the quick shifting of moods and attitudes being a basic characteristic that indicates a need for change. Versatility is the remarkable Gemini attribute. It is the capacity to investigate, perform, and relate over great areas for short periods of time and thus to connect all areas. It is mastery of design and perception, the power to conceptualize and create by putting elements together—people, colors, patterns. It is the reporter's mind, plus a brilliant ability to see things in objective, colorful arrangement. Strength lies in constant refreshment of outlook and joyful participation in all aspects of life.

Gemini is involvement with neighbors, family and relatives, telephones, arteries of news and communication—anything that enhances the human capacity for communication and self-expression. It is active, positive, and energetic, with an insatiable hunger for human interchange. Through Gemini bright and dark sides of personality merge and the mind has wings. As it flies it reflects the light of a boundless shining intellect. It is the development of varied talents from recognition of the duality of self.

Gemini is geared toward enjoying life to the fullest by finding, above all else, a means of expressing the inner self to the outside world.

CANCER
The Sign of the Crab

Cancer is the special relationship to home and involvement with the family unit. Maintaining harmony in the domestic sphere or improving conditions there is a major characteristic in this sector of the Zodiac. Cancer is attachment between two beings vibrating in sympathy with one another.

It is the comfort of a loving embrace, a tender generosity. Cancer is the place of shelter whenever there are lost or hungry souls in the night. Through Cancer we are fed, protected, comforted, and soothed. When the coldness of the world threatens, Cancer is there with gentle understanding. It is protection and understated loyalty, a medium of rich, living feeling that is both psychic and mystical. Highly intuitive, Cancer has knowledge that other signs do not possess. It is the wisdom of the soul.

It prefers the quiet contentment of the home and hearth to the busy search for earthly success and civilized pleasures. Still, there is a respect for worldly knowledge. Celebration of life comes through food. The sign is the muted light of warmth, security, and gladness, and its presence means nourishment. It rules fertility and the instinct to populate and raise young. It is growth of the soul. It is the ebb and flow of all our tides of feeling, involvements, habits, and customs.

Through Cancer is reflected the inner condition of all human beings, and therein lies the seed of knowledge out of which the soul will grow.

LEO
The Sign of the Lion

Leo is love. It represents the warmth, strength, and regeneration we feel through love. It is the radiance of life-giving light and the center of all attention and activity. It is passion, romance, adventure, and games. Pleasure, amusement, fun, and entertainment are all part of Leo. Based on the capacity for creative feeling and the desire to express love, Leo is the premier sign. It represents the unlimited outpouring of all that is warm and positive.

It is loyalty, dignity, responsibility, and command. Pride and nobility belong to Leo, and the dashing image of the knight in shining armor, of the hero, is part of Leo. It is a sense of high honor and kingly generosity born out of deep, noble love. It is the excitement of the sportsman, with all the unbeatable flair and style of success. It is a strong, unyielding will and true sense of personal justice, a respect for human freedom, and an enlightened awareness of people's needs.

Leo is involvement in the Self's awareness of personal talents and the desire and need to express them. At best it is forthrightness, courage and efficiency, authority and dignity, showmanship, and a talent for organization. Dependable and ardent, the Lion is characterized by individuality, positivism, and integrity.

It is the embodiment of human maturity, the effective individual in society, a virile creative force able to take chances and win. It is the love of laughter and the joy of making others happy. Decisive and enthusiastic, the Lion is the creative producer of the Zodiac It is the potential to light the way for others.

VIRGO
The Sign of the Virgin

Virgo is the sign of work and service. It is the symbol of the farmer at harvest time, and represents tireless efforts for the benefit of humanity, the joy of bringing the fruits of the Earth to the table of mankind. Celebration through work is the characteristic of this sign.

Sincerity, zeal, discipline, and devotion mark the sign of the Virgin.

The key word is purity, and in Virgo lies a potential for unlimited self-mastery. Virgo is the embodiment of perfected skill and refined talent. The thread of work is woven into the entire life of Virgo. All creativity is poured into streamlining a job, classifying a system, eradicating unnecessary elements of pure analysis. The true Virgo genius is found in separating the wheat from the chaff.

Spartan simplicity characterizes this sign, and Virgo battles the war between order and disorder. The need to arrange, assimilate, and categorize is great; it is the symbol of the diagnostician, the nurse, and the healer. Criticism and analysis describe this sign—pure, incisive wisdom and a shy appreciation of life's joys. All is devoted to the attainment of perfection and the ideal of self-mastery.

Virgo is the sign of health and represents the physical body as a functioning symbol of the mental and spiritual planes. It is the state of healing the ills of the human being with natural, temperate living. It is maturation of the ego as it passes from a self-centered phase to its awareness and devotion to humanity.

It is humanitarian, pragmatic, and scientific, with boundless curiosity. Focus and clarity of mind are the strong points, while strength of purpose and shy reserve underlie the whole sign. There is separateness, aloofness, and solitude for this beacon of the Zodiac. As a lighthouse guides ships, so Virgo shines.

LIBRA
The Sign of the Scales

Libra is the sign of human relationship, marriage, equality, and justice. It symbolizes the need of one human being for another, the capacity to find light, warmth, and life-giving love in relationship to another human being. It is union on any level—mental, sexual, emotional, or business. It is self-extension in a desire to find a partner with whom to share our joys. It is the capacity to recognize the needs of others and to develop to the fullest our powers of diplomacy, good taste, and refinement.

Libra is harmony, grace, aesthetic sensibility, and the personification of the spirit of companionship. It represents the skill to maintain balances and the ability to share mutually all life's benefits, trials, crises, and blessings. Libra is mastery at anticipation of another's needs or reactions. It is the exercise of simple justice with impartial delicacy.

It is the need to relate, to find a major person, place, or thing to sustain us and draw out our attention. It is growth through becoming awakened to the outside world and other people. It is the union of two loving souls in honesty, equality, mutual cooperation, and mutual accord.

SCORPIO
The Sign of the Scorpion

Scorpio is the sign of dark intensity, swirling passion, and sexual magnetism. It is the thirst for survival and regeneration that are the bases of sexual orientation and the creative impulses for self-expression. No other sign has such a profound instinct for survival and reproduction. Out of the abyss of emotions come a thousand creations, each one possessing a life of its own.

Scorpio is completion, determination, and endurance, fortified with enough stamina to outlive any enemy. It is the pursuit of goals despite any threat, warning, or obstacle that might stand in the way. It simply cannot be stopped. It knows when to wait and when to proceed. It is the constant state of readiness, a vibrant living force that constantly pumps out its rhythm from the depths of being.

Secretive and intimate, Scorpio symbolizes the self-directed creature with a will of steel. It is the flaming desire to create, manipulate, and control with a magician's touch. But the most mysterious quality is the capacity for metamorphosis, or total transformation.

This represents supremacy in the battle with dark unseen forces. It is the state of being totally fearless—the embodiment of truth and courage. It symbolizes the human capacity to face all danger and emerge supreme, to heal oneself. As a caterpillar spins its way into the darkness of a cocoon, Scorpio faces the end of existence, says goodbye to an old way of life, and goes through a kind of death—or total change.

Then, amid the dread of uncertainty, something remarkable happens. From hopelessness or personal crisis a new individual emerges, like a magnificent butterfly leaving behind its cocoon. It is a human being completely transformed and victorious. This is Scorpio.

SAGITTARIUS
The Sign of the Archer

Sagittarius is the sign of adventure and a thousand and one new experiences. It is the cause and purpose of every new attempt at adventure or self-understanding. It is the embodiment of enthusiasm, search for truth, and love of wisdom. Hope and optimism characterize this section of the Zodiac, and it is the ability to leave the past behind and set out again with positive resilience and a happy, cheerful outlook.

It is intelligence and exuberance, youthful idealism, and the desire to expand all horizons. It is the constant hatching of dreams, the hunger for knowledge, travel and experience. The goal is exploration itself.

Sagittarius is generosity, humor, and goodness of nature, backed up by the momentum of great expectations. It symbolizes the ability of people to be back in the race after having the most serious spills over the biggest hurdles. It is a healthy, positive outlook and the capacity to meet each new moment with unaffected buoyancy.

At this point in the Zodiac, greater conscious understanding begins to develop self-awareness and self-acceptance. It is an Olympian capacity to look upon the bright side and to evolve that aspect of mind we call conscience.

CAPRICORN
The Sign of the Sea Goat

Capricorn is the sign of structure and physical law. It rules depth, focus, and concentration. It is the symbol of success through perseverance, happiness through profundity. It is victory over disruption, and finds reality in codes set up by society and culture. It is the perpetuation of useful, tested patterns and a desire to protect what has already been established.

It is cautious, conservative, conscious of the passage of time, yet ageless. The Goat symbolizes the incorporation of reason into living and depth into loving.

Stability, responsibility, and fruitfulness through loyalty color this sector of the Zodiac with an undeniable and irrepressible awareness of success, reputation, and honor. Capricorn is the culmination of our earthly dreams, the pinnacle of our worldly life.

It is introspection and enlightenment through serious contemplation of the Self and its position in the world. It is mastery of understanding and the realization of dreams.

Capricorn is a winter blossom, a born professional with an aim of harmony and justice, beauty, grace, and success. It is the well-constructed pyramid: perfect and beautiful, architecturally correct, mysteriously implacable, and hard to know. It is highly organized and built on precise foundations to last and last and last. It is practical, useful yet magnificent and dignified, signifying permanence and careful planning. Like a pyramid, Capricorn has thick impenetrable walls, complex passageways, and false corridors. Yet somewhere at the heart of this ordered structure is the spirit of a mighty ruler.

AQUARIUS
The Sign of the Water Bearer

Aquarius is the symbol of idealized free society. It is the herding instinct in man as a social animal. It is the collection of heterogeneous elements of human consciousness in coherent peaceful coexistence. Friendship, goodwill, and harmonious contact are Aquarius attributes. It is founded on the principle of individual freedom and the brotherly love and respect for the rights of all men and women on Earth.

It is strength of will and purpose, altruism, and love of human fellowship. It is the belief in spontaneity and free choice, in the openness to live in a spirit of harmony and cooperation—liberated from restriction, repression, and conventional codes of conduct. It is the brilliant capacity to assimilate information instantaneously at the last minute and translate that information into immediate creative action, and so the result is to live in unpredictability.

This is the progressive mind, the collective mind—groups of people getting together to celebrate life. Aquarius is the child of the future, the utopian working for the betterment of the human race. Funds, charities, seeking better cities and better living conditions for others, involvement in great forms of media or communication, science or research in the hope of joining mankind to his higher self—this is all Aquarius.

It is invention, genius, revolution, discovery—instantaneous breakthrough from limitations. It's a departure from convention, eccentricity, the unexpected development that changes the course of history. It is the discovery of people and all the arteries that join them together. Aquarius is adventure, curiosity, exotic and alien appeal. It pours the water of life and intelligence for all humanity to drink. It is humanism, community, and the element of surprise.

PISCES
The Sign of the Fishes

Pisces is faith—undistracted, patient, all-forgiving faith—and therein lies the Pisces capacity for discipline, endurance, and stamina.

It is imagination and other-worldliness, the condition

of living a foggy, uncertain realm of poetry, music, and fantasy. Passive and compassionate, this sector of the Zodiac symbolizes the belief in the inevitability of life. It represents the view of life that everything exists in waves, like the sea. All reality as we know it is a dream, a magic illusion that must ultimately be washed away. Tides pull this way and that, whirlpools and undercurrents sweep across the bottom of life's existence, but in Pisces there is total acceptance of all tides, all rhythms, all possibilities. It is the final resolution of all personal contradictions and all confusing paradoxes.

It is the search for truth and honesty, and the devotion to love, utterly and unquestionably. It is the desire to act with wisdom, kindness, and responsibility and to welcome humanity completely free from scorn, malice, discrimination, or prejudice. It is total, all-embracing, idealistic love. It is the acceptance of two sides of a question at once and love through sacrifice.

Pisces is beyond reality. We are here today, but may be gone tomorrow. Let the tide of circumstances carry you where it will, for nothing is forever. As all things come, so must they go. In the final reel, all things must pass away. It is deliverance from sorrow through surrender to the infinite. The emotions are as vast as the ocean, yet in the pain of confusion there is hope in the secret cell of one's own heart. Pisces symbolizes liberation from pain through love, faith, and forgiveness.

THE SIGNS AND
THEIR KEY WORDS

		Positive	Negative
ARIES	self	courage, initiative, pioneer instinct	brash rudeness, selfish impetuosity
TAURUS	money	endurance, loyalty, wealth	obstinacy, gluttony
GEMINI	mind	versatility, communication	capriciousness, unreliability
CANCER	family	sympathy, homing instinct	clannishness, childishness
LEO	children	love, authority, integrity	egotism, force
VIRGO	work	purity, industry, analysis	faultfinding, cynicism
LIBRA	marriage	harmony, justice	vacillation, superficiality
SCORPIO	sex	survival, regeneration	vengeance, discord
SAGITTARIUS	travel	optimism, higher learning	lawlessness, irresponsibility
CAPRICORN	career	depth, responsibility	narrowness, gloom
AQUARIUS	friends	humanity, genius	perverse unpredictability
PISCES	faith	spiritual love, universality	diffusion, escapism

THE ELEMENTS AND
THE QUALITIES OF THE SIGNS

Every sign has both an element and a quality associated with it. The element indicates the basic makeup of the sign, and the quality describes the kind of activity associated with each.

Element	Sign	Quality	Sign
Fire	Aries	Cardinal	Aries
	Leo		Libra
	Sagittarius		Cancer
			Capricorn
Earth	Taurus	Fixed	Taurus
	Virgo		Leo
	Capricorn		Scorpio
			Aquarius
Air	Gemini	Mutable	Gemini
	Libra		Virgo
	Aquarius		Sagittarius
			Pisces
Water	Cancer		
	Scorpio		
	Pisces		

Signs can be grouped together according to their element and quality. Signs of the same element share many basic traits in common. They tend to form stable configurations and ultimately harmonious relationships. Signs of the same quality are often less harmonious, but share many dynamic potentials for growth and profound fulfillment.

The following pages describe these sign groupings in more detail.

The Fire Signs

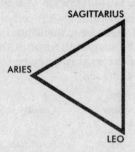

This is the fire group. On the whole these are emotional, volatile types, quick to anger, quick to forgive. They are adventurous, powerful people and act as a source of inspiration for everyone. They spark into action with immediate exuberant impulses. They are intelligent, self-involved, creative, and idealistic. They all share a certain vibrancy and glow that outwardly reflects an inner flame and passion for living.

The Earth Signs

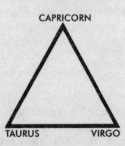

This is the earth group. They are in constant touch with the material world and tend to be conservative. Although they are all capable of spartan self-discipline, they are earthy, sensual people who are stimulated by the tangible, elegant, and luxurious. The thread of their lives is always practical, but they do fantasize and are often attracted to dark, mysterious, emotional people. They are like great cliffs overhanging the sea, forever married to the ocean but always resisting erosion from the dark, emotional forces that thunder at their feet.

The Air Signs

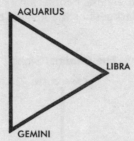

This is the air group. They are light, mental creatures desirous of contact, communication, and relationship. They are involved with people and the forming of ties on many levels. Original thinkers, they are the bearers of human news. Their language is their sense of word, color, style, and beauty. They provide an atmosphere suitable and pleasant for living. They add change and versatility to the scene, and it is through them that we can explore human intelligence and experience.

The Water Signs

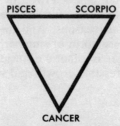

This is the water group. Through the water people, we are all joined together on emotional, nonverbal levels.

The water signs are silent, mysterious types whose magic hypnotizes even the most determined realist. They have uncanny perceptions about people and are as rich as the oceans when it comes to feeling, emotion, or imagination. They are sensitive, mystical creatures with memories that go back beyond time. Through water, life is sustained. These people have the potential for the depths of darkness or the heights of mysticism and art.

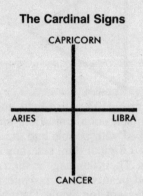

The Cardinal Signs

The cardinal signs present a picture of dynamism, activity, tremendous stress, and remarkable achievement. These people know the meaning of great change since their lives are often characterized by significant crises and major successes. The cardinal signs mark the beginning of the four seasons. And this combination is like a simultaneous storm of summer, fall, winter, and spring. The danger is chaotic diffusion of energy; the potential is irrepressible growth and victory.

The Fixed Signs

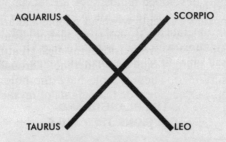

Fixed signs are always establishing themselves in a given place or area of experience. Like explorers who arrive and plant a flag, these people claim a position from which they do not enjoy being deposed. They are staunch, stalwart, upright, trusty, honorable people, although their obstinacy is well-known. Their contribution is fixity, and they are the angels who support our visible world.

The Mutable Signs

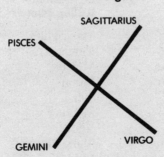

Mutable people are versatile, sensitive, intelligent, nervous, and deeply curious about life. They are the translators of all energy. They often carry out or complete tasks initiated by others. People from mutable signs have highly developed minds; they are imaginative and jumpy and think and talk a lot. At worst their lives are a Tower of Babel. At best they are adaptable and ready creatures who can assimilate one kind of experience and enjoy it while anticipating coming changes.

THE PLANETS AND THE SIGNS THEY RULE

The signs of the Zodiac are linked to the planets in the following way. Each sign is governed or ruled by one or more planets. No matter where the planets are located in the sky at any given moment, they still rule their respective signs. When they travel through the signs they rule, they have special dignity and their effects are stronger.

Following is a list of the planets and the signs they rule. After you read the definitions of the planets from pages 88 to 96, see if you can determine how the planet ruling *your* Sun sign has affected your life.

Signs	**Ruling Planets**
Aries	Mars, Pluto
Taurus	Venus
Gemini	Mercury
Cancer	Moon
Leo	Sun
Virgo	Mercury
Libra	Venus
Scorpio	Mars, Pluto
Sagittarius	Jupiter
Capricorn	Saturn
Aquarius	Saturn, Uranus
Pisces	Jupiter, Neptune

THE ZODIAC AND
THE HUMAN BODY

The signs of the Zodiac are linked to the human body in a direct relationship. Each sign has a part of the body with which it is associated.

It is traditionally believed that surgery is best performed when the Moon is passing through a sign *other* than the sign associated with the part of the body upon which an operation is to be performed. But often the presence of the Moon in a particular sign will bring the focus of attention to that very part of the body under medical scrutiny.

The principles of medical astrology are complex and beyond the scope of this introduction. We can, however, list the signs of the Zodiac and the parts of the human body connected with them. Once you learn these correspondences, you'll be amazed at how accurate they are.

Signs	Human Body
Aries	Head, brain, face, upper jaw
Taurus	Throat, neck, lower jaw
Gemini	Hands, arms, lungs, nerves
Cancer	Stomach, breasts, womb, liver
Leo	Heart, spine
Virgo	Intestines, liver
Libra	Kidneys, lower back
Scorpio	Sex and eliminative organs
Sagittarius	Hips, thighs, liver
Capricorn	Skin, bones, teeth, knees
Aquarius	Circulatory system, lower legs
Pisces	Feet, tone of being

THE ZODIACAL HOUSES
AND THE RISING SIGN

Apart from the month and day of birth, the exact time of birth is another vital factor in the determination of an accurate horoscope. Not only do planets move with great speed, but one must know how far the Earth has turned during the day. That way you can determine exactly where the planets are located with respect to the precise birthplace of an individual. This makes your horoscope *your* horoscope.

The horoscope sets up a kind of framework around which the life of an individual grows like wild ivy, this way and that, weaving its way around the trellis of the natal positions of the planets. The year of birth tells us the positions of the distant, slow-moving planets Jupiter, Saturn, Uranus, Neptune, and Pluto. The month of birth indicates the Sun sign, or birth sign as it is commonly called, as well as indicating the positions of the rapidly moving planets Venus, Mercury, and Mars. The day of birth, as well as the time, locates the position of our Moon. And the moment of birth—the exact hour and minute—determines the houses through what is called the Ascendant, or Rising sign.

The illustration on the next page shows the flat chart, or natural wheel, an astrologer uses. The inner circle of the wheel is labeled 1 through 12. These 12 divisions are known as the houses of the Zodiac.

The 1st house always starts from the position marked E, which corresponds to the eastern horizon. The rest of the houses 2 through 12 follow around in a "counterclockwise" direction. The point where each house starts is known as a cusp, or edge.

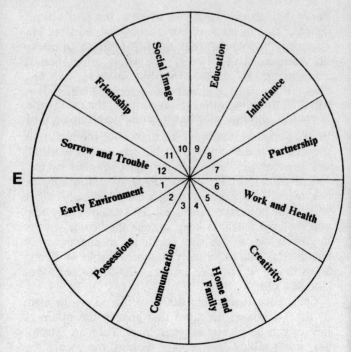

The 12 Houses of the Zodiac

The cusp, or edge, of the 1st house (point E) is where an astrologer would place your Rising sign, the Ascendant. The Rising sign is very important in a horoscope, as it defines your self-image, outlook, physical constitution, early environment, and whole orientation to life. And, as already mentioned, the exact time of your birth determines your Rising sign. Let's see how this works.

As the Earth rotates on its axis once every 24 hours, each one of the 12 signs of the Zodiac appears to be "rising" on the horizon, with a new one appearing about every two hours. Actually it is the turning of the

Earth that exposes each sign to view, but you will remember that in much of our astrological work we are discussing "apparent" motion. This Rising sign marks the Ascendant, and it colors the whole orientation of a horoscope. It indicates the sign governing the first house of the chart, and will thus determine which signs will govern all the other houses.

To visualize this idea, imagine two color wheels with twelve divisions superimposed upon each other. Just as the Zodiac is divided into twelve star groups (constellations) that we identify as the signs, another twelve-fold division is used to denote the houses. Now imagine one wheel (the signs) moving slowly while the other wheel (the houses) remains still. This analogy may help you see how the signs keep shifting the "color" of the houses as the Rising sign continues to change every two hours. But to simplify things, a Table of Rising Signs has been provided on pages 20–21 for your specific Sun sign.

Once your Rising sign has been placed on the cusp of the 1st house, the signs that govern the other 11 houses can be placed on your chart. Then an astrologer, using tables of planetary motion, can locate the positions of all the planets in their appropriate houses. The house where your Sun sign is describes your basic character and your fundamental drives. And the houses where the other planets are in your chart suggest the areas of life on Earth in which you will be most likely to focus your constant energy and center your activity.

The illustration on page 83 briefly identifies each of the 12 houses of the Zodiac. Now the pages that follow provide a detailed discussion of the meanings of the houses. In the section after the houses we will define all the known planets of the solar system, with a separate section on the Moon, in order to acquaint you with more of the astrological vocabulary you will be meeting again and again.

THE MEANING OF THE HOUSES

The twelve houses of every horoscope represent areas of life on Earth, or regions of worldly experience. Depending on which sign of the Zodiac was rising on the eastern horizon at the moment of birth, the activity of each house will be "colored" by the zodiacal sign on its cusp, or edge. In other words, the sign falling on the first house will determine what signs will fall on the rest of the houses.

1 The first house determines the basic orientation to all of life on Earth. It indicates the body type, face, head, and brain. It rules your self-image, or the way others see you because of the way you see your self. This is the Ascendant of the horoscope and is the focus of energies of your whole chart. It acts like a prism through which all of the planetary light passes and is reflected in your life. It colors your outlook and influences everything you do and see.

2 This is the house of finances. Here is your approach to money and materialism in general. It indicates where the best sources are for you to improve your financial condition and your earning power as a whole. It indicates chances for gain or loss. It describes your values, alliances, and assets.

3 This is the house of the day-to-day mind. Short trips, communication, and transportation are associated with this house. It deals with routines, brothers and sisters, relatives, neighbors, and the near environment at hand. Language, letters, and the tools for transmitting information are included in third-house matters.

4 This is the house that describes your home and home life, parents, and childhood in the sense of indicating the kind of roots you come from. It symbolizes your present home and domestic situation and reflects your need for privacy and retreat from the world, indicating, of course, what kind of scene you require.

5 Pleasure, love affairs, amusements, parties, creativity, children. This is the house of passion and courtship and of expressing your talents, whatever they are. It is related to the development of your personal life and the capacity to express feeling and enjoy romance.

6 This is the house of work. Here there are tasks to be accomplished and maladjustments to be corrected. It is the house of health as well, and describes some of the likely places where physical health difficulties may appear. It rules routines, regimen, necessary jobs as opposed to a chosen career, army, navy, police—people employed, co-workers, and those in service to others. It indicates the individual's ability to harvest the fruit of his own efforts.

7 This is the house of marriage, partnership, and unions. It represents the alter ego, all people other than yourself, open confrontation with the public. It describes your partner and the condition of partnership as you discern it. In short, it is your "take" on the world. It indicates your capacity to make the transition from courtship to marriage and specifically what you seek out in others.

8 This is the house of deep personal transition, sex as a form of mutual surrender and interchange between human beings. It is the release from tensions and the completion of the creative processes. The eighth house also has to do with taxes, inheritances, and the finances of others, as well as death as the ending of cycles and crises.

9 This is the house of the higher mind, philosophy, religion, and the expression of personal conscience through moral codes. It indicates political leanings, ethical views, and the capacity of the individual for a broader perspective and deeper understanding of himself in relation to society. It is through the ninth house that you make great strides in learning and travel to distant places and come to know yourself through study, dreams, and wide experience.

10 This is the house of career, honor, and prestige. It marks the culmination of worldly experience and indicates the highest point you can reach, what you look up to, and how high you can go in this lifetime. It describes your parents, employers, and how you view authority figures, the condition and direction of your profession, and your position in the community.

11 This is the house of friendships. It describes your social behavior, your views on humanity, and your hopes, aspirations, and wishes for an ideal life. It will indicate what kinds of groups, clubs, organizations, and friendships you tend to form and what you seek out in your chosen alliances other than with your mate or siblings. This house suggests the capacity for the freedom and unconventionality that an individual is seeking, his sense of his connection with mankind, and the definition of his goals, personal and social.

12 This is the house of seclusion, secret wisdom, and self-incarceration. It indicates our secret enemies as well, in the sense that there may be persons, feelings, or memories we are trying to escape. It is self-undoing in that this house acts against the ego in order to find a higher, more universal purpose. It rules prisons, hospitals, charities, and selfless service. It is the house of unfinished psychic business.

THE PLANETS OF THE SOLAR SYSTEM

The planets of the solar system all travel around the Sun at different speeds and different distances. Taken with the Sun, they all distribute individual intelligence and ability throughout the entire chart.

The planets modify the influence of the Sun in a chart according to their own particular natures, strengths, and positions. Their positions must be calculated for each year and day, and their function and expression in a horoscope will change as they move from one area of the Zodiac to another.

Following, you will find brief statements of their pure meanings.

THE SUN

The Sun is the center of existence. Around this flaming sphere all the planets revolve in endless orbits. Our star is constantly sending out its beams of light and energy without which no life on Earth would be possible. In astrology it symbolizes everything we are trying to become, the center around which all of our activity in life will always revolve. It is the symbol of our basic nature and describes the natural and constant thread that runs through everything that we do from birth to death on this planet.

Everything in the horoscope ultimately revolves around this singular body. Although other forces may be prominent in the charts of some individuals, still the

THE SUN

Sun is the total nucleus of being and symbolizes the complete potential of every human being alive. It is vitality and the life force. Your whole essence comes from the position of the Sun.

You are always trying to express the Sun according to its position by house and sign. Possibility for all development is found in the Sun, and it marks the fundamental character of your personal radiations all around you.

It symbolizes strength, vigor, ardor, generosity, and the ability to function effectively as a mature individual and a creative force in society. It is consciousness of the gift of life. The undeveloped solar nature is arrogant pushy, undependable, and proud, and is constantly using force.

MERCURY

Mercury is the planet closest to the Sun. It races around our star, gathering information and translating it to the rest of the system. Mercury represents your capacity to understand the desires of your own will and to translate those desires into action.

MERCURY

In other words it is the planet of mind and the power of communication. Through Mercury we develop an ability to think, write, speak, and observe—to become aware of the world around us. It colors our attitudes and vision of the world, as well as our capacity to communicate our inner responses to the outside world. Some people who have serious disabilities in their power of verbal communication have often wrongly been described as people lacking intelligence.

Although this planet (and its position in the horoscope) indicates your power to communicate your thoughts and perceptions to the world, intelligence is something deeper. Intelligence is distributed throughout all the planets. It is the relationship of the planets to each other that truly describes what we call intelligence. Mercury rules speaking, language, mathematics, draft and design, students, messengers, young people, offices, teachers, and any pursuits where the mind of man has wings.

VENUS

Venus is beauty. It symbolizes the harmony and radiance of a rare and elusive quality: beauty itself. It is refinement and delicacy, softness and charm. In astrology it indicates grace, balance, and the aesthetic sense. Where Venus is we see beauty, a gentle drawing in of energy and the need for satisfaction and completion. It is a special touch that finishes off rough edges.

VENUS

Venus is the planet of sensitivity and affection, and it is always the place for that other elusive phenomenon: love. Venus describes our sense of what is beautiful and loving. Poorly developed, it is vulgar, tasteless, and self-indulgent. But its ideal is the flame of spiritual love—Aphrodite, goddess of love, and the sweetness and power of personal beauty.

MARS

Mars is raw, crude energy. The planet next to Earth but outward from the Sun is a fiery red sphere that charges through the horoscope with force and fury. It represents the way you reach out for new adventure and new experience. It is energy drive, initiative, courage, daring. It is the power to start something and see it through. It can be thoughtless, cruel and wild, angry and hostile, causing cuts, burns, scalds, wounds. It can stab its way through a chart, or it can be the symbol of healthy spirited adventure, well-channeled constructive power to begin and keep up the drive.

MARS

If you have trouble starting things, if you lack the get-up-and-go to start the ball rolling, if you lack aggressiveness and self-confidence, chances are there's another planet influencing your Mars. Mars rules soldiers, butchers, surgeons, salespeople—in general any field that requires daring, bold skill, operational technique, or self-promotion.

JUPITER

Jupiter is the largest planet of the solar system. Planet Jupiter rules good luck and good cheer, health, wealth, optimism, happiness, success, joy. It is the symbol of opportunity and always opens the way for new possibilities in your life. It rules exuberance, enthusiasm, wisdom, knowledge, generosity, and all forms of expansion in general. It rules actors, statesmen, clerics, professional people, religion, publishing, and the distribution of many people over large areas.

♃

JUPITER

Sometimes Jupiter makes you think you deserve everything, and you become sloppy, wasteful, careless and rude, prodigal and lawless, in the illusion that nothing can ever go wrong. Then there is the danger of your showing overconfidence, exaggeration, undependability, and overindulgence.

Jupiter is the minimization of limitation and the emphasis on spirituality and potential. It is the thirst for knowledge and higher learning.

SATURN

Saturn circles our system in dark splendor with its mysterious rings, forcing us to be awakened to whatever we have neglected in the past. It will present real puzzles and problems to be solved, causing delays, obstacles, and hindrances. By doing so, Saturn stirs our own sensitivity to those areas where we are laziest.

SATURN

Here we must patiently develop method, and only through painstaking effort can our ends be achieved. It brings order to a horoscope and imposes reason just where we are feeling least reasonable. By creating limitations and boundary, Saturn shows the consequences of being human and demands that we accept the changing cycles inevitable in human life. Saturn rules time, old age, and sobriety. It can bring depression, gloom, jealousy, and greed, or serious acceptance of responsibilities out of which success will develop. With Saturn there is nothing to do but face facts. It rules laborers, stones, granite, rocks, and crystals.

THE OUTER PLANETS: URANUS, NEPTUNE, PLUTO

Uranus, Neptune, and Pluto are the outer planets. They liberate human beings from cultural conditioning, and in that sense are the lawbreakers. In early times it was thought that Saturn was the last planet of the solar system—the outer limit beyond which we could never go. The discovery of the next three planets beyond Saturn ushered in new phases of human history, revolution, and technology.

URANUS

Uranus rules unexpected change, upheaval, revolution. It is the symbol of total independence and asserts the freedom of an individual from all restriction and restraint. It is a breakthrough planet and indicates talent, originality, and genius in a horoscope. It usually causes last-minute reversals and changes of plan, unwanted separations, accidents, catastrophes, and eccentric behavior. It can add irrational rebelliousness and perverse bohemianism to a personality or a streak of unaffected brilliance in science and art.

URANUS

Uranus rules technology, aviation, and all forms of electrical and electronic advancement. It governs great leaps forward and topsy-turvy situations, and always turns things around at the last minute. Its effects are difficult to predict, since it rules sudden last-minute decisions and events that come like lightning out of the blue.

NEPTUNE

Neptune dissolves existing reality the way the sea erodes the cliffs beside it. Its effects are subtle like the ringing of a buoy's bell in the fog. It suggests a reality higher than definition can usually describe. It awakens a sense of higher responsibility often causing guilt, worry, anxieties, or delusions. Neptune is associated with all forms of escape and can make things seem a certain way so convincingly that you are absolutely sure of something that eventually turns out to be quite different.

NEPTUNE

It is the planet of illusion and therefore governs the invisible realms that lie beyond our ordinary minds, beyond our simple factual ability to prove what is "real." Treachery, deceit, disillusionment, and disappointment are linked to Neptune. It describes a vague reality that promises eternity and the divine, yet in a manner so complex that we cannot really fathom it at all. At its worst Neptune is a cheap intoxicant; at its best it is the poetry, music, and inspiration of the higher planes of spiritual love. It has dominion over movies, photographs, and much of the arts.

PLUTO

Pluto lies at the outpost of our system and therefore rules finality in a horoscope—the final closing of chapters in your life, the passing of major milestones and points of development from which there is no return. It is a final wipeout, a closeout, an evacuation. It is a subtle but powerful catalyst in all transformations that occur. It creates, destroys, then recreates. Sometimes Pluto starts its influence with a minor event or insignificant incident that might even go unnoticed. Slowly but surely, little by little, everything changes, until at last there has been a total transformation in the area of your life where Pluto has been operating. It rules mass thinking and the trends that society first rejects, then adopts, and finally outgrows.

PLUTO

Pluto rules the dead and the underworld—all the powerful forces of creation and destruction that go on all the time beneath, around, and above us. It can bring a lust for power with strong obsessions.

It is the planet that rules the metamorphosis of the caterpillar into a butterfly, for it symbolizes the capacity to change totally and forever a person's lifestyle, way of thought, and behavior.

THE MOON

Exactly how does the Moon affect us psychologically and psychically? We know it controls the tides. We understand how it affects blood rhythm and body tides, together with all the chemical fluids that constitute our physical selves. Astronauts have walked upon its surface, and our scientists are now studying and analyzing data that will help determine the age of our satellite, its origin, and makeup.

THE MOON

But the true mystery of that small body as it circles our Earth each month remains hidden. Is it really a dead, lifeless body that has no light or heat of its own, reflecting only what the gigantic Sun throws toward it? Is it a sensitive reflecting device, which translates the blinding, billowing energy from our star into a language our bodies can understand?

In astrology, the Moon is said to rule our feelings, customs, habits, and moods. As the Sun is the constant, ever shining source of life in daytime, the Moon is our nighttime mother, lighting up the night and swiftly moving, reflecting ever so rapidly the changing phases of behavior and personality. If we feel happy or joyous, or we notice certain habits and repetitive feelings that bubble up from our dark centers then vanish as quickly as they appeared, very often it is the position of the Moon that describes these changes.

THE MOON IN ALL SIGNS

The Moon moves quickly through the Zodiac, that is, through all twelve signs of our Sun's apparent path. It stays in each sign for about 2¼ days. During its brief stay in a given sign, the moods and responses of people are always colored by the nature of that sign, any planets located there at that time, or any other heavenly bodies placed in such a way that the Moon will pick up their "vibration" as well. It's astonishing to observe how clearly the Moon changes people's interests and involvements as it moves along.

The following section gives brief descriptions of the Moon's influence in each sign.

MOON IN ARIES

There's excitement in the air. Some new little thing appears, and people are quick and full of energy and enterprise, ready for something new and turning on to a new experience. There's not much patience or hesitation, doubt or preoccupation with guilty self-damning recriminations. What's needed is action. People feel like putting their plans into operation. Pleasure and adventure characterize the mood, and it's time for things to change, pick up, improve. Confidence, optimism, positive feeling pervade the air. Sick people take a turn for the better. Life stirs with a feeling of renewal. People react bravely to challenges, with a sense of courage and dynamism. Self-reliance is the key word, and people minimize their problems and maximize the power to exercise freedom of the will. There is an air of abruptness and shortness of consideration, as people are feeling the courage of their convictions to do something for themselves. Feelings are strong and intuitive, and the mood is idealistic and freedom-oriented.

MOON IN TAURUS

Here the mood is just as pleasure loving, but less idealistic. Now the concerns are more materialistic, money-oriented, down-to-earth. The mood is stable, diligent, thoughtful, deliberate. It is a time when feelings are rich and deep, with a profound appreciation of the good things the world has to offer and the pleasures of the sensations. It is a period when people's minds are serious, realistic, and devoted to the increases and improvements of property and possessions and acquisition of wealth. There is a conservative tone, and people are fixed in their views, needing to add to their stability in every way. Assessment of assets, criticism, and the execution of tasks are strong involvements of the Taurus Moon when financial matters demand attention. It is devotion to security on a financial and emotional level. It is a fertile time, when ideas can begin to take root and grow.

MOON IN GEMINI

There is a rapid increase in movement. People are going places, exchanging ideas and information. Gossip and news travel fast under a Gemini Moon, because people are naturally involved with communication, finding out things from some, passing on information to others. Feelings shift to a mental level now, and people feel and say things that are sincere at the moment but lack the root and depth to endure much beyond the moment. People are involved with short-term engagements, quick trips. There is a definite need for changing the scene. You'll find people flirtatious and talkative, experimental and easygoing, falling into encounters they hadn't planned on. The mind is quick and active, with powers of writing and speaking greatly enhanced. Radio, television, letters, newspapers, magazines are in the spotlight with the Moon in Gemini, and new chances pop up for self-expression, with new people involved. Relatives and neighbors are tuned in to you and you to them. Take advantage of this fluidity of mind. It can rescue you from worldly involvements and get you into new surroundings for a short while.

MOON IN CANCER

Now you'll see people heading home. People turn their attention inward to their place of residence under a Cancer Moon. The active, changeable moods of yesterday vanish, and people settle in as if they were searching for a nest of security. Actually people are retiring, seeking to find peace and quiet within themselves. That's what they're feeling when they prefer to stay home rather than go out with a crowd of people to strange places. They need the warmth and comfort of the family and hearth. Maybe they feel anxious and insecure from the hustle and bustle of the workaday world. Maybe they're just tired. But it's definitely a time of tender need for emotional sustenance. It's a time for nostalgia and returning to times and places that once nourished deeply. Thoughts of parents, family, and old associations come to people. The heritage of their family ties holds them strongly now. These are personal needs that must be fed. Moods are deep and mysterious and sometimes sad. People are silent, psychic, and imaginative during this period. It's a fruitful time when people respond to love, food, and all the comforts of the inner world.

MOON IN LEO

The shift is back out in the world, and people are born again, like kids. They feel zestful, passionate, exuberant and need plenty of attention. They're interested in having a good time, enjoying themselves, and the world of entertainment takes over for a while. Places of amusement, theaters, parties, sprees, a whole gala of glamorous events, characterize this stage of the Moon's travel. Gracious, lavish hosting and a general feeling of buoyancy and flamboyance are in the air. It's a time of sunny, youthful fun when people are in the mood to take chances and win. The approach is direct, ardent, and strong. Bossy, authoritarian feelings predominate, and people throw themselves forward for all they're worth. Flattery is rampant, but the ego is vibrant and flourishing with the kiss of life, romance, and love. Speculation is indicated, and it's usually a time to go out and try your hand at love. Life is full and rich as a summer meadow, and feelings are warm.

MOON IN VIRGO

The party's over. Eyelashes are on the table. This is a time for cleaning up after the merrymakers have gone home. People are now concerned with sobering up and getting personal affairs straight, clearing up any confusions or undefined feelings from the night before, and generally attending to the practical business of doctoring up after the party. People are back at work, concerned with necessary, perhaps tedious tasks—paying bills, fixing and adjusting things, and generally purifying their lives, streamlining their affairs, and involving themselves with work and service to the community. Purity is the key word in personal habits, diet, and emotional needs. Propriety and coolness take the place of yesterday's devil-may-care passion, and the results are a detached, inhibited period under a Virgo

Moon. Feelings are not omitted; they are merely subjected to the scrutiny of the mind and thus purified. Health comes to the fore, and people are interested in clearing up problems.

MOON IN LIBRA

Here there is a mood of harmony, when people strive to join with other people in a bond of peace and justice. At this time people need relationships and often seek the company of others in a smooth-flowing feeling of love, beauty, and togetherness. People make efforts to understand other people, and though it's not the best time to make decisions, many situations keep presenting themselves from the outside to change plans and offer new opportunities. There is a general search for accord between partners, and differences are explored as similarities are shared. The tone is concilatory, and the mood is one of cooperation, patience, and tolerance. People do not generally feel independent, and sometimes this need to share or lean on others disturbs them. It shouldn't. This is the moment for uniting and sharing, for feeling a mutual flow of kindness and tenderness between people. The air is ingratiating and sometimes lacks stamina, courage, and a consistent, definite point of view. But it is a time favoring the condition of beauty and the development of all forms of art.

MOON IN SCORPIO

This is not a mood of sharing. It's driving, intense, brooding—full of passion and desire. Its baser aspects are the impulses of selfishness, cruelty, and the pursuit of animal drives and appetites. There is a craving for excitement and a desire to battle and win in a bloodthirsty war for survival. It is competitive and ruthless, sarcastic and easily bruised, highly sexual and touchy, without being especially tender. Retaliation, jealousy, and revenge can be felt too during this time. Financial involvements, debts, and property issues arise now. Powerful underworld forces are at work here, and great care is needed to transform ignorance into wisdom, to keep the mind from descending into the lower depths. During the Moon's stay in Scorpio we contact the dark undercurrents swirling around and get in touch with a magical part of our natures. Interest lies in death, inheritance, and the powers of rebirth and regeneration.

MOON IN SAGITTARIUS

Here the mind climbs out of the depths, and people are involved with the higher, more enlightened, and conscious facets of their personality. There's a renewed interest in learning, education, and philosophy, and a new involvement with ethics, morals, national and international issues: a concern with looking for a better way to live. It's a time of general improvement, with people feeling more deeply hopeful and optimistic. They are dreaming of new places, new possibilities, new horizons. They are emerging from the abyss and leaving the past behind, with their eyes gazing toward the new horizon. They decide to travel, or renew their contacts with those far away. They question their religious beliefs and investigate new areas of metaphysical inquiry. It's a time for adventure, sports, playing the field—people have their eye on new possibilities. They are bored with depression and details. They feel restless and optimistic, joyous and delighted to be alive. Thoughts revolve around adventure, travel, liberation.

MOON IN CAPRICORN

When the Moon moves into Capricorn, things slow down considerably. People require a quiet, organized, and regularized condition. Their minds are sober and realistic, and they are methodically going about bringing their dreams and plans into reality. They are more conscious of what is standing between them and success, and during this time they take definite, decisive steps to remove any obstacles from their path. They are cautious, suspicious, sometimes depressed, discouraged, and gloomy, but they are more determined than ever to accomplish their tasks. They take care of responsibilities now, wake up to facts, and wrestle with problems and dilemmas of this world. They are politically minded and concerned with social convention now, and it is under a Capricorn Moon that conditioning and conformity elicit the greatest responses. People are moderate and serious and surround themselves with what is most familiar. They want predictable situations and need time to think deeply and deliberately about all issues. It's a time for planning.

MOON IN AQUARIUS

Spontaneity replaces the sober predictability of yesterday. Now events, people, and situations pop up, and you take advantage of unsought opportunities and can expect the unexpected. Surprises, reversals, and shifts in plans mark this period. There is a resurgence of optimism, and things you wouldn't expect to happen suddenly do. What you were absolutely sure was going to happen simply doesn't. Here there is a need for adventure born from a healthy curiosity that characterizes people's moods. Unrealistic utopias are dreamed of, and it is from such idealistic dreams that worlds of the future are built. There is a renewed interest in friendship, comradeship, community, and union on high planes of mental and spiritual companionship. People free each other from grudges or long-standing deadlocks, and there is a hopeful joining of hands in a spirit of love and peace. People don't feel like sticking to previous plans, and they must be able to respond to new situations at the last minute. People need freedom. Groups of people come together and meet, perhaps for a common purpose of having dinner or hearing music, and leave knowing each other better.

MOON IN PISCES

Flashes of brilliant insight and mysterious knowledge characterize the Moon's passage in Pisces. Sometimes valuable "truths" seem to emerge which, later in the light of day, turn out to be false. This is a time of poetry, intuition, and music, when worldly realities can be the most illusory and unreliable of all. There are often feelings of remorse, guilt, or sorrow connected with a Pisces Moon—sorrow from the childhood or family or past. Confusion, anxiety, worry, and a host of imagined pains and sorrows may drag you down until you cannot move or think. Often there are connections with hospitals, prisons, alcohol, drugs, and lower forms of escape. It is a highly emotional time, when the feelings and compassion for humanity and all people everywhere rise to the surface of your being. Mysteries of society and the soul now rise to demand solutions, but often the riddles posed during this period have many answers that all seem right. It is more a time for inner reflection than positive action. It is a time when poetry and music float to the surface of the being, and for the creative artist it is the richest source of inspiration.

MOON TABLES

CORRECTION FOR NEW YORK TIME, FIVE HOURS WEST OF GREENWICH

Atlanta, Boston, Detroit, Miami, Washington,
Montreal, Ottawa, Toronto, Bogota,
Havana, Lima, Santiago...................... Same time

Chicago, New Orleans, Houston, Winnipeg,
Churchill, Mexico City .... Deduct 1 hour

Albuquerque, Denver, Phoenix, El Paso,
Edmonton, Helena....................... Deduct 2 hours

Los Angeles, San Francisco, Reno,
Portland, Seattle, Vancouver .... Deduct 3 hours

Honolulu, Anchorage, Fairbanks, Kodiak... Deduct 5 hours

Nome, Samoa, Tonga, Midway .... Deduct 6 hours

Halifax, Bermuda, San Juan, Caracas,
La Paz, Barbados ....Add 1 hour

St. John's, Brasilia, Rio de Janeiro,
Sao Paulo, Buenos Aires, Montevideo....... Add 2 hours

Azores, Cape Verde Islands.................... Add 3 hours

Canary Islands, Madeira, Reykjavik .... Add 4 hours

London, Paris, Amsterdam, Madrid, Lisbon,
Gibraltar, Belfast, Rabat .... Add 5 hours

Frankfurt, Rome, Oslo, Stockholm, Prague,
Belgrade..................................... Add 6 hours

Bucharest, Beirut, Tel Aviv, Athens, Istanbul,
Cairo, Cape Town, Johannesburg .... Add 7 hours

Moscow, Leningrad, Baghdad, Addis Ababa,
Dhahran, Nairobi, Teheran, Zanzibar .... Add 8 hours

Bombay, Calcutta, Sri Lanka .... Add 10 ½ hours

Hong Kong, Shanghai, Manila, Peking,
Perth .... Add 13 hours

Tokyo, Okinawa, Darwin, Pusan .... Add 14 hours

Sydney, Melbourne, Port Moresby, Guam .... Add 15 hours

Auckland, Wellington, Suva, Wake........... Add 17 hours

1998 MOON SIGN DATES—NEW YORK TIME

JANUARY		FEBRUARY		MARCH	
Day Moon Enters		**Day Moon Enters**		**Day Moon Enters**	
1. Aquar.		1. Aries		1. Aries	
2. Pisces	4:57 am	2. Taurus	4:26 pm	2. Taurus	0:01 am
3. Pisces		3. Taurus		3. Taurus	
4. Aries	7:44 am	4. Gemini	8:10 pm	4. Gemini	2:16 am
5. Aries		5. Gemini		5. Gemini	
6. Taurus	10:53 am	6. Gemini		6. Cancer	7:28 am
7. Taurus		7. Cancer	1:58 am	7. Cancer	
8. Gemini	2:43 pm	8. Cancer		8. Leo	3:47 pm
9. Gemini		9. Leo	9:58 am	9. Leo	
10. Cancer	7:44 pm	10. Leo		10. Leo	
11. Cancer		11. Virgo	8:10 pm	11. Virgo	2:36 am
12. Cancer		12. Virgo		12. Virgo	
13. Leo	2:46 am	13. Virgo		13. Libra	2:59 pm
14. Leo		14. Libra	8:18 am	14. Libra	
15. Virgo	0:32 pm	15. Libra		15. Libra	
16. Virgo		16. Scorp.	9:14 pm	16. Scorp.	3:52 am
17. Virgo		17. Scorp.		17. Scorp.	
18. Libra	0:45 am	18. Scorp.		18. Sagitt.	3:57 pm
19. Libra		19. Sagitt.	8:57 am	19. Sagitt.	
20. Scorp.	1:35 pm	20. Sagitt.		20. Sagitt.	
21. Scorp.		21. Capric.	5:31 pm	21. Capric.	1:44 am
22. Scorp.		22. Capric.		22. Capric.	
23. Sagitt.	0:26 am	23. Aquar.	10:11 pm	23. Aquar.	8:02 am
24. Sagitt.		24. Aquar.		24. Aquar.	
25. Capric.	7:40 am	25. Pisces	11:43 pm	25. Pisces	10:44 am
26. Capric.		26. Pisces		26. Pisces	
27. Aquar.	11:28 am	27. Aries	11:43 pm	27. Aries	10:50 am
28. Aquar.		28. Aries		28. Aries	
29. Pisces	1:09 pm			29. Taurus	10:07 am
30. Pisces				30. Taurus	
31. Aries	2:22 pm			31. Gemini	10:39 am

Summer time to be considered where applicable.

1998 MOON SIGN DATES—NEW YORK TIME

APRIL Day Moon Enters		MAY Day Moon Enters		JUNE Day Moon Enters	
1. Gemini		1. Cancer		1. Virgo	
2. Cancer	2:11 pm	2. Leo	4:50 am	2. Virgo	
3. Cancer		3. Leo		3. Libra	10:18 am
4. Leo	9:37 pm	4. Virgo	2:48 pm	4. Libra	
5. Leo		5. Virgo		5. Scorp.	11:07 pm
6. Leo		6. Virgo		6. Scorp.	
7. Virgo	8:26 am	7. Libra	3:20 am	7. Scorp.	
8. Virgo		8. Libra		8. Sagitt.	10:35 am
9. Libra	9:05 pm	9. Scorp.	4:11 pm	9. Sagitt.	
10. Libra		10. Scorp.		10. Capric.	7:51 pm
11. Libra		11. Scorp.		11. Capric.	
12. Scorp.	9:57 am	12. Sagitt.	3:49 am	12. Capric.	
13. Scorp.		13. Sagitt.		13. Aquar.	3:04 am
14. Sagitt.	9:53 pm	14. Capric.	1:40 pm	14. Aquar.	
15. Sagitt.		15. Capric.		15. Pisces	8:32 am
16. Sagitt.		16. Aquar.	9:31 pm	16. Pisces	
17. Capric.	8:06 am	17. Aquar.		17. Aries	0:24 pm
18. Capric.		18. Aquar.		18. Aries	
19. Aquar.	3:42 pm	19. Pisces	3:04 am	19. Taurus	2:48 pm
20. Aquar.		20. Pisces		20. Taurus	
21. Pisces	8:07 pm	21. Aries	6:07 am	21. Gemini	4:27 pm
22. Pisces		22. Aries		22. Gemini	
23. Aries	9:31 pm	23. Taurus	7:07 am	23. Cancer	6:40 pm
24. Aries		24. Taurus		24. Cancer	
25. Taurus	9:10 pm	25. Gemini	7:26 am	25. Leo	11:05 pm
26. Taurus		26. Gemini		26. Leo	
27. Gemini	8:56 pm	27. Cancer	8:59 am	27. Leo	
28. Gemini		28. Cancer		28. Virgo	6:55 am
29. Cancer	10:58 pm	29. Leo	1:39 pm	29. Virgo	
30. Cancer		30. Leo		30. Libra	6:06 pm
		31. Virgo	10:22 pm		

Summer time to be considered where applicable.

1998 MOON SIGN DATES—NEW YORK TIME

JULY Day Moon Enters		AUGUST Day Moon Enters		SEPTEMBER Day Moon Enters	
1. Libra		1. Scorp.		1. Capric.	
2. Libra		2. Sagitt.	2:49 am	2. Capric.	
3. Scorp.	6:46 am	3. Sagitt.		3. Aquar.	4:22 am
4. Scorp.		4. Capric.	0:19 pm	4. Aquar.	
5. Sagitt.	6:25 pm	5. Capric.		5. Pisces	7:49 am
6. Sagitt.		6. Aquar.	6:32 pm	6. Pisces	
7. Sagitt.		7. Aquar.		7. Aries	8:53 am
8. Capric.	3:28 am	8. Pisces	10:05 pm	8. Aries	
9. Capric.		9. Pisces		9. Taurus	9:17 am
10. Aquar.	9:53 am	10. Pisces		10. Taurus	
11. Aquar.		11. Aries	0:11 am	11. Gemini	10:41 am
12. Pisces	2:23 pm	12. Aries		12. Gemini	
13. Pisces		13. Taurus	2:05 am	13. Cancer	2:21 pm
14. Aries	5:46 pm	14. Taurus		14. Cancer	
15. Aries		15. Gemini	4:47 am	15. Leo	8:49 pm
16. Taurus	8:34 pm	16. Gemini		16. Leo	
17. Taurus		17. Cancer	1:56 am	17. Leo	
18. Gemini	11:19 pm	18. Cancer		18. Virgo	5:53 am
19. Gemini		19. Leo	3:02 pm	19. Virgo	
20. Gemini		20. Leo		20. Libra	4:58 pm
21. Cancer	2:44 am	21. Virgo	11:22 pm	21. Libra	
22. Cancer		22. Virgo		22. Libra	
23. Leo	7:50 am	23. Virgo		23. Scorp.	5:23 am
24. Leo		24. Libra	10:03 am	24. Scorp.	
25. Virgo	3:35 pm	25. Libra		25. Sagitt.	6:06 pm
26. Virgo		26. Scorp.	10:26 pm	26. Sagitt.	
27. Virgo		27. Scorp.		27. Sagitt.	
28. Libra	2:15 am	28. Scorp.		28. Capric.	5:31 am
29. Libra		29. Sagitt.	10:56 am	29. Capric.	
30. Scorp.	2:45 pm	30. Sagitt.		30. Aquar.	1:54 pm
31. Scorp.		31. Capric.	9:24 pm		

Summer time to be considered where applicable.

1998 MOON SIGN DATES—NEW YORK TIME

OCTOBER		NOVEMBER		DECEMBER	
Day Moon Enters		**Day Moon Enters**		**Day Moon Enters**	
1. Aquar.		1. Aries	6:28 am	1. Taurus	
2. Pisces	6:24 pm	2. Aries		2. Gemini	4:31 pm
3. Pisces		3. Taurus	6:13 am	3. Gemini	
4. Aries	7:33 pm	4. Taurus		4. Cancer	4:29 pm
5. Aries		5. Gemini	5:12 am	5. Cancer	
6. Taurus	6:58 pm	6. Gemini		6. Leo	6:56 pm
7. Taurus		7. Cancer	5:40 am	7. Leo	
8. Gemini	6:45 pm	8. Cancer		8. Leo	
9. Gemini		9. Leo	9:34 am	9. Virgo	1:22 am
10. Cancer	8:49 pm	10. Leo		10. Virgo	
11. Cancer		11. Virgo	5:38 pm	11. Libra	11:14 am
12. Cancer		12. Virgo		12. Libra	
13. Leo	2:26 am	13. Virgo		13. Libra	
14. Leo		14. Libra	4:59 am	14. Scorp.	0:17 am
15. Virgo	11:33 am	15. Libra		15. Scorp.	
16. Virgo		16. Scorp.	5:42 pm	16. Sagitt.	0:48 pm
17. Libra	11:03 pm	17. Scorp.		17. Sagitt.	
18. Libra		18. Scorp.		18. Capric.	11:56 pm
19. Libra		19. Sagitt.	6:14 am	19. Capric.	
20. Scorp.	11:37 am	20. Sagitt.		20. Capric.	
21. Scorp.		21. Capric.	5:46 am	21. Aquar.	9:18 am
22. Scorp.		22. Capric.		22. Aquar.	
23. Sagitt.	0:17 am	23. Capric.		23. Pisces	4:46 pm
24. Sagitt.		24. Aquar.	3:44 am	24. Pisces	
25. Capric.	0:06 pm	25. Aquar.		25. Aries	10:05 pm
26. Capric.		26. Pisces	11:15 am	26. Aries	
27. Aquar.	9:45 pm	27. Pisces		27. Aries	
28. Aquar.		28. Aries	3:35 pm	28. Taurus	1:06 am
29. Aquar.		29. Aries		29. Taurus	
30. Pisces	3:59 am	30. Taurus	4:54 pm	30. Gemini	2:23 am
31. Pisces				31. Gemini	

Summer time to be considered where applicable.

1998 FISHING GUIDE

	Good	Best
January	5-9-10-13-14-15-28	11-12-20
February	9-10-11-12-13-14	3-8
March	5-10-11-12-13-28	14-15-16-21
April	8-9-19	3-10-11-12-13-14-26
May	3-12-13-14-25	8-9-10-11-19
June	2-8-9-10-13-17	7-11-12-24
July	6-7-10-11-12-16-23	1-8-9-31
August	7-8-11-22-30	5-6-9-10-14
September	3-4-5-7-8-9-13-20-28	6
October	2-5-6-28	3-4-7-8-12-20
November	1-2-3-5-6-7-11-19-30	4-27
December	2-3-4-10-18-26	1-5-6

1998 PLANTING GUIDE

	Aboveground Crops	Root Crops
January	2-3-7-11-30	18-19-20-21-22-26
February	3-4-7-8-27	15-16-17-18-22-23
March	2-3-7-11-12-30	14-15-16-17-21-22-26
April	3-4-10-11-27-30	12-13-14-18-22-23
May	1-7-8-9-10-28	15-16-19-20-24
June	4-5-6-7-24-25	11-12-16-20
July	1-2-3-4-5-8-28-29-30-31	13-17-18-21-22
August	1-5-6-25-26-27-28	9-10-13-14-18
September	1-2-21-22-23-24-25-29	10-14-15
October	3-4-21-22-26-27-30-31	7-8-11-12-18-19
November	22-23-27	4-8-14-15-16-17-18
December	1-19-20-24-25-28-29	5-6-12-13-14-15

	Pruning	Weeds and Pests
January	21-22	13-14-15-16-17-23-24
February	17-18	12-13-20-21-24-25
March	16-17-26	19-20-24
April	13-14-22-23	15-16-20-21-24-25
May	19-20	12-13-17-18-22
June	16	10-13-14-18-22-23
July	13-21-22	11-15-16-19-20
August	9-10-18	8-11-12-15-16-20-21
September	14-15	8-12-16-17-18-19
October	11-12	6-9-10-13-14-15-16-17
November	8-17-18	6-10-11-12-13
December	5-6-14-15	7-8-9-10-17-18

1998 PHASES OF THE MOON—NEW YORK TIME

New Moon	First Quarter	Full Moon	Last Quarter
Dec. 29 ('97)	Jan. 5	Jan. 12	Jan. 20
Jan. 28	Feb. 3	Feb. 11	Feb. 19
Feb. 26	Mar. 5	Mar. 12	Mar. 21
Mar. 27	Apr. 3	Apr. 11	Apr. 19
Apr. 26	May 3	May 11	May 18
May 25	June 1	June 9	June 17
June 23	July 1	July 9	July 16
July 23	July 31	Aug. 7	Aug. 14
Aug. 21	Aug. 30	Sept. 6	Sept. 12
Sept. 20	Sept. 28	Oct. 5	Oct. 12
Oct. 20	Oct. 28	Nov. 4	Nov. 10
Nov. 28	Nov. 26	Dec. 13	Dec. 10
Dec. 18	Dec. 26	Jan. 1 ('99)	Jan. 9 ('99)

Each phase of the Moon lasts approximately seven to eight days, during which the Moon's shape gradually changes as it comes out of one phase and goes into the next.

There will be a partial solar eclipse during the New Moon phase on February 26 and August 21.

Use the Moon phases to connect you with your lucky numbers for this year. See the next page (page 112) and your lucky numbers.

LUCKY NUMBERS
FOR SCORPIO: 1998

Lucky numbers and astrology can be linked through the movements of the Moon. Each phase of the thirteen Moon cycles vibrates with a sequence of numbers for your Sign of the Zodiac over the course of the year. Using your lucky numbers is a fun system that connects you with tradition.

New Moon	First Quarter	Full Moon	Last Quarter
Dec. 29 ('97) 9 6 1 4	Jan. 5 4 5 8 7	Jan. 12 7 7 2 9	Jan. 20 4 0 8 5
Jan. 28 2 6 9 1	Feb. 3 1 4 3 3	Feb. 11 8 7 9 0	Feb. 19 9 2 8 5
Feb. 26 9 3 4 7	March 5 7 6 1 0	March 12 3 7 3 4	March 21 1 0 7 2
March 27 5 0 6 9	April 3 8 8 3 5	April 11 5 0 9 4	April 19 7 4 8 2
April 26 3 6 5 5	May 3 5 9 2 0	May 11 0 1 7 4	May 18 8 2 1 2
May 25 5 4 4 8	June 1 8 1 0 9	June 9 4 6 3 1	June 17 7 2 5 1
June 23 1 1 0 5	July 1 7 0 6 3	July 9 1 9 4 7	July 16 8 2 1 9
July 23 4 6 1 0	July 31 0 1 5 2	August 7 7 3 6 7	August 14 7 1 0 9
August 21 4 8 0 5	August 30 9 6 3 7	Sept. 6 2 1 2 5	Sept. 12 4 4 8 9
Sept. 20 1 2 6 0	Sept. 28 1 4 8 2	Oct. 5 5 3 6 5	Oct. 12 5 5 9 2
Oct. 20 9 1 4 5	Oct. 28 7 2 5 6	Nov. 4 6 0 9 8	Nov. 10 8 3 5 0
Nov. 18 0 4 4 1	Nov. 26 5 8 9 0	Dec. 3 9 0 2 6	Dec. 10 6 8 3 7
Dec. 18 7 4 6 1	Dec. 26 0 4 5 8	Jan. 1 ('99) 8 7 2 4	Jan. 9 ('99) 4 8 3 9

SCORPIO
YEARLY FORECAST: 1998

Forecast for 1998 Concerning Business
Prospects, Financial Affairs, Health,
Travel, Employment, Love and Marriage
for Persons Born with the Sun
Sun in the Zodiacal Sign of Scorpio,
October 23–November 22.

This year promises to be a full and satisfying one for those of you born under the influence of the Sun in the zodiacal sign of Scorpio. Scorpio is ruled by Mars, the planet of dynamism and initiative, and Pluto, the planet of transformation. These influences will inspire you to focus your energies and ambitions on those events and situations that will help you reach your most desired goals. Direction and determination are among Scorpio's strongest attributes. You are bound to use them in the coming year to attain personal and professional ambitions. You must take care, however, that in your urge for self-expression and creativity, you do not become rigid and narrow. Use Scorpio's talents of knowing when to wait and when to proceed to overcome any obstacles that seem to stand in your way. In your business and professional life, you will sometimes feel behind the competition. Determine this year to take a leaf from their books and you can find yourself brimming with new and innovative ideas. A key to greater success may be too look beyond your immediate surroundings. Movement and change are likely to be major factors in your success. Financially, you can be on an even keel. But you will probably have to work a little harder to streamline your budget. Opportunities to boost future financial resources will be within your grasp. You only need to look within yourself to discover the talents and resources you have to make the most of whatever comes your way. This is likely to be the year when you will feel more physically fit. Avoid taking advantage of your good health, however. It is one thing to maintain health, it is another to improve your fitness. Pay attention to your body, and it will let you know its needs. Personal relationships are of more than usual importance to you this year. You are likely to be more aware of the value of older friendships. A social whirl to meet new people will not be too appealing. The year can be fulfilling romantically but major commitments may not be in the stars in 1998.

Whatever your profession may be, you could make great strides in advancing your ambitions. You will be very perceptive in evaluating the opportunities that come your way. Efforts you make to impress those who can give support are sure to be rewarded. You have an innate talent for recognizing when to press forward and when to be patient. Scorpio's tendency to secrecy is likely at times to tempt you to be less than forthcoming. This can be an advantage or a disadvantage. You will probably have to make some tough decisions in alliances along the way. Be prepared for challenges but know that you have the endurance to overcome them. It will not be difficult for Scorpio to persevere in 1998. Routine work this coming year could require you to focus your energies more than in the past. It appears that you could let ordinary tasks slide in favor of grand projects. Make every effort to overcome this temptation. This is a year during which you should be more aware of the need to delegate. You could take on more responsibilities than you can comfortably handle. Scorpio wants to be on top of every situation if possible. Keep reminding yourself that others can be of great value in easing the burdens. If you are an employer, the year promises benefits to your company through the efforts of its workers. It will be up to you, however, to encourage and motivate your employees. If you set an example, you can expect loyalty and increased efforts on their part. Self-employed Scorpio is likely to be on the right track in 1998. A program of promotion and publicity can pay off. Some past contacts may come out of the blue with offers. New clients will find your work impressive and could come through with lucrative offers. You might find yourself with more work than you can handle. Try not to have too many irons in the fire, however. It will be too difficult to concentrate if your energies are diffused.

The year ahead will likely be more reassuring financially. Expect opportunities to increase your income. The key to your success is to explore your skills and talents and put them to the best use. An offer for additional work that you enjoy doing can be the inspiration. This could be the spur to investigating a whole new line of work that will help ensure future financial security. Keep on top of your bank book, however. This does not seem to be the year for spending on large-ticket items. You will feel safer if you can be assured you have plenty for a rainy day. Joint ventures and investments may prove more profitable than you expected. Property transactions will require careful negotiations on your part. Where others may be involved, you could become entangled in disrupting wrangles over details. This is the time to stick to your guns. Avoid entering into risky speculation in 1998. You will know which schemes are not for you. If you are undecided, do not be too proud to ask for professional advice.

Be careful about neglecting your well-being in 1998. Good health and control of your own body are important to Scorpio. You are quite capable of sticking to a good diet. But you can slack off when you are rushed or feel you are too busy. When the year begins, draw up a diet plan and stick to it. Keeping fit through exercise will invigorate you physically and mentally. A health club may not be for you. But you can find activities that suit your age and condition. Whatever you select this year, it would be wise to consult a doctor or physical trainer to make sure you are going in the right direction. Even though this promises to be a busy year, find time for relaxation and rest. Try to make weekends as free as possible so that you can renew your energies.

Travel this year will probably be confined to more immediate surroundings. Journeys abroad or far afield do not appear to be in the cards. You could, however, think of planning a long trip for the future. If you do, this is the year to make the arrangements and talk to others who might want to join you. Business travel is likely to prove fruitful. You can learn more than you expected and conclude deals to your satisfaction. Closer to home, short trips and outings will be more to your liking. There will be times when trips to see others will be of importance to you. Attending family reunions or special occasions are the chance to renew relationships and even mend some fences.

Personal relationships may have some ups and downs in 1998, but overall, you will find great pleasure in your friendships. This is likely to be a year in which you find old friends more congenial than new ones. You may not even want to meet too many new people. Someone who was once close but drifted away may reappear in your life. If there were problems in the past, they are likely to seem minor now. You will find that both you and the other person have matured in understanding and considerateness. Circumstances this year may draw you and your family closer together. Past misunderstandings and conflicts can be forgotten in a spirit of forgiving and forgetting. You can make a great deal of difference yourself by your willingness to make the first moves toward a closer relationship.

The coming year is likely to find you with greater insight into your own emotions. Scorpio is intense about love and romance and often demands the same commitment in return. It appears you are beginning to realize that love is not always perfect. You will discover that you can make the compromises necessary to make your relationships lasting and fulfilling. For married or attached Scorpio, the partnership will evolve into a greater stability and emotional security. If you have children, they will be a source of inspiration and encouragement for you and your spouse to set examples. Single Scorpio is not likely to be disappointed if a life-long partner does not appear on the horizon. You are more than likely to think twice about someone who offers romance rather than friendship. It appears that you are more determined in the coming year to pursue personal and career priorities. Securing your future and preparing yourself for whatever challenges come your way will make 1998 a banner year for Scorpio.

SCORPIO DAILY FORECAST: 1998

1st Week/January 1–7

Thursday January 1st. On this first day of the new year, Scorpio can take pride in recent accomplishments. You will likely spend time thinking about plans for your personal life and your work in the months ahead. If you are involved in festivities, whether as a host or guest, let your glamorous side show. Those around you will revel in your charms.

Friday the 2nd. Money matters require extra care today. You may be tempted by sales and want to splurge on bargains. Be sure, however, that you are buying genuine bargains. Moreover, think about your pocketbook and whether you have the cash to spare. If you are uncertain about a romantic involvement, it is likely this is the time to think the situation through rationally.

Saturday the 3rd. Double-check social arrangements. This is a day when you could end up in the wrong place at the wrong time if you are not careful. Single Scorpio could have a tough time deciding whether or not the words of an attractive smooth talker are genuine. Be wary, and take what you hear with a grain of salt.

Sunday the 4th. Leisure and entertainment activities are highlighted today. Relax and have some fun in your spare time. You probably will not have to go very far in order to enjoy yourself. Local gatherings are likely to be stimulating. Children can have fun on an outing if weather permits. You might plan some creative indoor activities for the whole family.

Monday the 5th. Try not to be too ruthless if you are clearing up around the home or office today. You could end up putting something valuable in the trash because you think you will not need it later. Clothes in particular deserve a second glance. Look carefully at records and documents. A neighbor's invitation is likely to be worth accepting.

Tuesday the 6th. Be careful about messages you receive that seem a bit vague. Wires can get crossed easily if details are not specific. Documents need careful attention, especially the small print. Your partner seems to be going through ups and downs. Try to be supportive. If you are single, avoid pushing too hard with a new romantic interest. A real estate opportunity could arise.

Wednesday the 7th. You and your partner probably will not see eye-to-eye when discussing domestic issues. Leave any major plans you want to put into action until the dust has settled a little. A neighbor or relative may intervene in a dispute that is getting out of hand. Listen to advice you get. By the end of the day, you will probably owe someone a favor.

Weekly Summary

The first week of 1998 finds Scorpio looking forward to a year of personal and career fulfillment. A temporary struggle to make ends meet can probably be settled through the intervention of someone close to you. Avoid getting carried away with spending, however, simply because an issue has been resolved for the time being. Determine to look to the future.

Joint finances and business concerns are looking more healthy. If you are thinking of making a real estate deal, just the right opportunity could come up this week. Important documents, such as contracts, deserve a very thorough reading.

Romance tends to be a bit rocky. If you are looking forward to a date with someone new, be sure to get the details of time and place clear. Ending up in the wrong place at the wrong time could make you think you have been stood up. For Scorpio still waiting for a date, be cautious in trusting someone new too quickly. Take your time in making a decision. The weekend is a time for relaxing more and simply enjoying the good things in life.

2nd Week/January 8–14

Thursday the 8th. Troubles in your domestic life and close relationships are likely to be resolved today. You have more energy to put into business matters. This is a favorable time for increasing involvement in joint ventures. If you want to attract new clients, think about a creative entertainment or offer a gift incentive to get them interested.

Friday the 9th. Choosing the right place is likely to be a key factor in influencing a business deal. If you are planning to take part in a trade show, be sure that it is located where the majority of your market operates. A professional conference can put you in touch with colleagues who have new ideas. Discuss home improvements with your partner. He or she will appreciate your attentiveness.

Saturday the 10th. Money matters are likely to be up and down today. You may be able to save on the weekly shopping, but you could make a mistake on a major purchase. Give yourself a chance to sleep on your decision before going ahead. Some of those around you have a habit of letting you down when you least expect it. Try to forgive and forget.

Sunday the 11th. Do not build up your expectations too much today in relation to a trip you have planned. For one reason or another, it could turn out to be disappointing. Revive everyone's energy, including your own, by indulging in an activity you all enjoy. If you are staying at home, set yourself only a few small tasks to complete.

Monday the 12th. Restless urges seem to be keeping you on the move at the moment. Any change of scene is likely to be beneficial. Get detailed or complicated work and routine responsibilities out of the way early in the day. The Full Moon in your sign brings a confident outlook now. Use it to influence business matters in a key meeting.

Tuesday the 13th. Meetings with influential people are favored now. You might not be able to complete a business agreement just yet, but you can lay some excellent groundwork. Be prepared to make last-minute changes if a client or your boss requires them. Home life could be potentially erratic. Avoid confrontation, and try to do something relaxing.

Wednesday the 14th. You should be able to consolidate recent efforts at work today. Complicated and intricate tasks can be gotten through faster than you expect if you put your mind to it. Catch up on routine tasks such as filing and routine correspondence. If you are thinking about carving out a new career path, consider work of a technical or practical nature.

Weekly Summary

Ongoing problems that have been plaguing domestic life are likely to improve this week. It is not in your interest to spend too much time laboring over tasks that keep you confined in one place. You will probably need a change of scene during or just after the weekend. Getting away from everything that is routine will prove to be a good tonic for Scorpio who is feeling stressed.

Business matters can be especially productive this week. Not all arrangements will be completed, but you will make excellent headway. Boosting business will require meeting the demands of your market. Creative efforts can be the key to reaching your goals. Extra research could be helpful too. Opportunities may arise to set you on a new career path.

Personal finances need care. Although you may be able to save in some areas, you could end up being penny-wise and pound-foolish. You can avoid this through proper planning. Benefits come your way when you think long and hard about major purchases.

3rd Week/January 15–21

Thursday the 15th. This is a day for turning to friends for inspiration. You are likely to be faced with a number of opportunities to make new contacts. Strike while the iron is hot. A new associate will probably become increasingly important to you in the future. Put your mind to it, and you can fulfill one of your cherished personal desires.

Friday the 16th. This should be a productive day where work matters are concerned. You are likely to get the best results by becoming involved in team efforts. Scorpio's social life appears to be looking up. You probably will not have to go very far to find some stimulating entertainment. If you are new to your neighborhood, accept any invitations that come your way.

Saturday the 17th. Concentrate on your most personal dreams and schemes today. It is likely that you will do something concrete and get the ball rolling. Relaxation is part of your key to success. When you take time to rest and think, you can come up with innovative ideas. Time spent in a faraway retreat could be refreshing. Share the time with a loved one.

Sunday the 18th. Privacy is always important to Scorpio, and never more than today. You do not want those around you poking into your personal affairs. Be sure, however, you are not tactless in maintaining your privacy. In a romantic involvement, you would be wise to play your cards close to your chest. You need to know more about the other person's intentions.

Monday the 19th. Do not pay too much attention to rumors circulating around the workplace. There is probably not a lot of truth in them. For Scorpio who has been temporarily out of work, avoid any stress. This is a day when you can benefit much more by resting and clearing your mind than by becoming anxious about the future.

Tuesday the 20th. Family members are likely to be more open to discussing matters that lately have been swept under the rug. Where work is concerned, today you will realize that there is no gain without pain. You may have to put forward a lot of effort, but you will be pleased with the results in the long run. Later, aim to take life more slowly.

Wednesday the 21st. If you are staying home today, noisy neighbors are likely to get on your nerves. You may not be in the mood for a confrontation, however. Try to shut out their noise with noise you prefer to hear. Play some of your favorite music, but wear headphones rather than launch a counterattack if you want to keep the peace.

Weekly Summary

Friends and acquaintances are likely to be an inspiration this week. You will probably be surprised at how friendly some new neighbors can be. There is no need to be suspicious or concerned about their approaches. Enjoy invitations that are offered. With other neighbors, you could find problems with noise. It would be best to avoid dealing with the situation head-on at the moment.

New contacts are likely to be made both in your social life and in the business world. It may not be obvious at the moment, but chances are that new people you are introduced to now can be influential in the future. Group efforts appear to help you get ahead with outstanding matters on the job front.

A special wish or dream stands a good chance of being realized this week. The weekend is the best time to focus on your private hopes. It is likely to be when you are at your most restful that you manage to dream up the perfect way to achieve your goals. Getting away from the usual surroundings can benefit you physically and mentally.

4th Week/January 22–28

Thursday the 22nd. This is a day for following closely your own intuition. Where business matters are concerned, an important contact is likely to be made. Plans may not necessarily be completed, but they can be moved a step forward. Home life is probably going to be a little bumpy. Try not to get involved in a hot dispute with your partner since arguments may lead nowhere.

Friday the 23rd. Be thrifty with your spending. Efforts put into doing your homework in relation to a business venture should start to pay off now. There is likely to be a breakthrough in negotiations for a contract you are hoping to sign soon. Put your faith in business colleagues whom you consider to be forward thinking. Their ideas can inspire your creative side.

Saturday the 24th. This is a good day for catching up on personal accounts. Balance the household budget. Take stock of staple supplies to be sure that you are not running out of anything vital. You should have a fairly peaceful day. Take your time over a decision concerning financial investments. You would probably be wise to check out alternatives.

Sunday the 25th. You will probably feel quite restless today. Spend some time getting out to see other people. If you are just becoming acquainted with your neighbors, it might be the right time to issue a cordial invitation. Long-distance journeys are favored. Being in a different environment is certain to be stimulating.

Monday the 26th. Do not be afraid to reach out to other people today. The signs are favorable for getting in touch with a variety of friends and associates. Finalize arrangements. Get going on correspondence that has been needing your attention for some time. Try to save routine tasks until another day when you are feeling more practical.

Tuesday the 27th. Before you make a commitment, be sure that you understand what is involved in a new business venture you are eager to get started on. Look after your prized possessions if you are going to be out in the public arena today. Scorpio who is in the world of antiques can find this a better day for buying than for selling.

Wednesday the 28th. You should be able to make good progress with a current project today. By avoiding distractions, you could even finish the job. Where business and property matters are concerned, it is likely that an important document will be signed. On the domestic front, concentrate on finishing up small jobs that need doing.

Weekly Summary

You are wise to trust your instincts and inspirations this week, both in business and in your personal life. Any inkling that it is not worth getting into a heavy argument at home is likely to be on target. There are sure to be much better ways to use your energies. Any storms that appear to be developing may not come to much if you do not contribute to them.

You should be able to make considerable progress in the business world. Nevertheless, you still need to be patient, since it may take others involved a while to make up their minds and give a firm commitment. New contacts are likely to be important in meeting your goals. It is a good idea to research your subject thoroughly.

Try to be careful where spending is concerned. Efforts to balance the books at home and in your personal account should be helpful. If necessary, ask for professional help. It is wiser to know exactly where you stand than to go spending blindly. If a problem is developing, at least you can nip it in the bud. When it comes to investments, it will probably be worth putting off any decisions until you have more information.

5th Week/January 29–February 4

Thursday the 29th. Be careful not to overdo it with projects you have already begun. You could end up getting out less than you put in. Take a look at what else you want to achieve for the future and spend some time focusing on those goals. Emotionally, you are likely to be on a roller coaster. If you are looking for a new partner, you could attract a real firecracker.

Friday the 30th. Young people are likely to be a source of inspiration. Give some serious thought to turning a hobby into a business venture. Beauty and jewelry products are likely to be lucrative items if you are in sales. Make a point of socializing more. Contacts you can make could prove invaluable in one way or another.

Saturday the 31st. Promotion and marketing appear to be your keys to success in the business world. This is especially true if you are self-employed or hoping to turn a pleasurable pastime into a money-earning enterprise. This is a favorable day for taking children out to enjoy themselves in a theme park or in a similar activity.

Sunday February 1st. Although you can get a lot done today, it would not be wise to completely wear yourself out in the process. Remember that this is traditionally a day of rest. Take a flyer and accept an invitation to a social function that seems appealing. There is no real reason for missing out on a little fun.

Monday the 2nd. It is likely to be difficult to pin down your partner to specific plans today. Stick instead to making your own plans. Good progress can be made with work projects. The increased cooperation of colleagues is likely to be helpful in this respect. If you are out of work, follow up old leads and make new applications with updated information.

Tuesday the 3rd. Do not expect life to be completely harmonious on the home front. It is likely that you and a partner will disagree on one particular issue. Try to just let it ride while your loved one seems to be in a contrary frame of mind. Coldness from other people is never pleasant. However, try not to take other people's preoccupations too personally.

Wednesday the 4th. The fog does not appear to be lifting on the domestic scene. Although you may feel a little alienated, the situation will probably not affect you so much if you get going and do your own thing. Friends have a habit of being tactless at the moment. Try not to pay too much attention to what they say. Neighbors and relatives seem to be better company.

Weekly Summary

It is important this week to maintain the right balance between work and play, as well as work and rest. You have a tendency at this time to overdo things and to get carried away once you get absorbed in a task. You can make excellent progress, but too much fussing to achieve perfection could end up being pointless and a waste of time.

This is a key week for planning for the future. If you are thinking of making a career change, moving into self-employment is a distinct possibility. It could be possible to turn a stimulating pastime into a money-making proposition. Focus more on marketing than on trying to make your product necessarily different or better. Attracting clientele in the first place is likely to be your key to success. You can work on fine-tuning later on.

Home life could be a little up and down this week. It tends to be best to leave partners to their own devices to some extent. You could feel a bit left out of your loved one's plans. This will probably only be a temporary situation, however. For single Scorpio, this is not the most fruitful of times to try and meet a new partner. Just relax.

6th Week/February 5–11

Thursday the 5th. Look before you leap today. It is not a good idea to jump in and make a major commitment if your thoughts have not had time to develop. A business venture that intrigues you could actually be quite dubious when you take the time to investigate it further. You and your friends may not see to eye-to-eye. Trust your own judgment.

Friday the 6th. It looks as though many of the difficulties that have made life hard during the past few days are beginning to be resolved. Some are disappearing altogether. Now is a good time for clearing any deadwood out of your life. Clear out unused clothes from your closet. The better your surroundings are arranged, the more organized you are likely to feel. Looking over a budget situation now will prevent problems in the future.

Saturday the 7th. A break from your usual environment is likely to be stimulating. Forget about routines and get involved in new activities or visit or a new place. A trip to the countryside can stimulate you physically and mentally. Getting back to nature is an opportunity to clear your mind of passing worries. Perhaps plan a family get-together with loved ones who have been absent for a while.

Sunday the 8th. It probably will not be so easy to simply switch off from routine affairs today. If you are away from home, it is likely you will feel happier cutting short a break. That way you can return early and get organized for the week ahead. A surprise visit or call from a friend or acquaintance could fill you in on some gossip.

Monday the 9th. You are probably not feeling too sure of yourself today. Put off making major decisions or commitments until you feel your feet are on more solid ground. An interesting-looking proposal needs close investigation. All may not be as it seems. Resolve to improve your diet and exercise regimen. It can boost your mental outlook.

Tuesday the 10th. Try not to get into an argument with your boss or someone else in authority. You may not see eye-to-eye about the best way to get a job done, but it is possible that he or she actually has some better ideas. If you feel you need more support from others to complete the work, this is a good time to say so and get your requirements met.

Wednesday the 11th. Work commitments and personal interests need to be carefully balanced today. Although there may be a lot to take care of in your personal life, it is best to make private telephone calls when you are at home. Maintaining a professional image at work is to your advantage now. Aim to stay in your boss's good graces.

Weekly Summary

This is a week for clearing some of the deadwood out of your life before making any further moves forward. This applies as much to your personal relationships as to your home and work environments. There seems little point in holding onto relationships and situations that are not proving to be fulfilling.

A change of scene is likely to be a real tonic. You are entering a new phase at the weekend, when it is particularly beneficial to get into a different environment. From this point on it is preferable to look at ways of broadening your horizons. New educational interests can be as stimulating as traveling to a different environment.

Treat new business schemes with caution. Some deception may be involved, although it may not be an intentional effort to pull the wool over your eyes. Good progress can be made at work if you manage to keep on the right side of a superior. Greater support with difficult tasks should be available if you need it. Try to keep your private life separate from your professional life. Your personal or family budget needs more attention.

7th Week/February 12–18

Thursday the 12th. This is not a good day for getting involved in financial setups with friends, even though you may be encouraged to. If you feel you cannot back out, it is a good idea to set up the arrangement on a formal basis. Ask for all the details in writing. A business deal you have been hoping to bring off is likely to come to fruition today.

Friday the 13th. Scorpio can look forward to a happy and congenial day where social life is concerned.

Friendships in particular will be especially rewarding. This is a favorable time for meeting new people and making new friends. For single Scorpio, it is also a key time for meeting a new romantic partner. Get out and about and you can create the opportunity.

Saturday the 14th. Allow yourself a lot of time alone this weekend. You need to benefit from thinking and planning without too many distractions. Get going on finishing chores that have been neglected before they get any worse. There is no real reason to feel guilty about shutting out the outside world. Those around you understand you have to have your own space now.

Sunday the 15th. Expect a full and busy day. Friends or family have plans that include you. An outing to the theater or a museum could be on the agenda. A responsibility you feel obliged to meet is likely to take some time. Anxious feelings about a loved one could put your emotions in a turmoil. The advice of a friend or relative may be just the thing to put your mind at rest.

Monday the 16th. You appear to be getting off to a good start on the work front. Success is apt to be yours as well if you are looking for new career avenues. Repayment of a loan may present you with a pleasant surprise. Be wary of financial advice from a distant source. You probably do not have enough information.

Tuesday the 17th. This may not be the easiest day for making important decisions. You probably are not feeling too sure of yourself. Get basics in place before making any major moves. Background research is likely to be helpful. If there are domestic problems, do your best to work through them. Others who are involved may be expecting you to take the initiative.

Wednesday the 18th. Confidence in your own abilities can be renewed today. Others' support of your plans and decisions will be a source of encouragement. Moving forward with assurance could be the key to achieving a personal goal. Attention to your image will pay off if you determine to improve your diet and your exercise regimen. You might be thinking of joining a health club.

Weekly Summary

Scorpio can seek and achieve a happy balance this week. Social events appear to be fulfilling, especially if you are spending more time with friends. You will probably also need plenty of time alone, however. The early part of the weekend is probably the best time for relaxing and making the most of the chance to recharge your batteries.

Beware of getting involved in complicated financial or business schemes with friends or neighbors. If you are in sales, avoid the temptation to try and promote your business by selling to people you know socially. Business and pleasure are not a favorable mix this week. New financial schemes you may be interested in require more background research.

A lack of decisiveness could slow down your progress early in the week. Concentrate first on clearing up neglected work rather than beginning new projects. Later on, your self-confidence is likely to return. Expect a superior to be behind you all the way. Others around you appear to be supportive and encouraging of your efforts at self-improvement.

8th Week/February 19–25

Thursday the 19th. Love and money are unlikely to mix happily. Keep any discussion about joint finances lighthearted and easygoing. Even for the most determined Scorpio, if a romance seems to be too costly on your time, money, and energy, this could be the time to call it a day. Vacillating will not resolve any conflicting emotions you may have.

Friday the 20th. Be single-minded in your approach to the main issues of the day. Generally, this is not difficult for Scorpio. If a joint financial or business investment intrigues you, get all the details from others involved. It is likely that someone you have had your eye on for a while will make the first move.

Saturday the 21st. This is an excellent day for setting goals. You have the determination now to achieve what you set out to do. Grasp an opportunity to complete an ongoing project. Others are supportive. Take time to enjoy socializing. This could be the time to mix business with pleasure. Be open to unusual invitations that come your way.

Sunday the 22nd. Those around you could upset your plans today. Be prepared for an unexpected visit from a relative or neighbor. Keep an eye on time. Certain arrangements you have made could take more time than you expect. You might have been neglecting someone close to you. Let him or her know you do care. Arrange a quiet time together.

Monday the 23rd. Sitting still will accomplish little, especially for self-employed Scorpio. The time is favorable for making new contacts and consolidating recent ones. Travel could be involved. If so, be sure arrangements are in order. A friend's problems could intrude on your schedule. If you do not have time to listen, be sympathetic but firm.

Tuesday the 24th. Financial difficulties you have been struggling with should come to a head today. Their solution does not seem to be too far off. Be careful about spending on entertainment. Your personal budget could be overextended. Tie up a few loose ends today. A major project at work can be finished. Enlist the help of colleagues if necessary.

Wednesday the 25th. Negotiations involving property or legal matters are likely to prove fruitful and bring a deal to a conclusion. Your efforts could mean a profit. Past attempts to cultivate a particular friendship or association appear to be paying off. Make the most of your good fortune by extending an invitation.

Weekly Summary

It is still advisable to do background research if you are thinking of entering into a new business arrangement, particularly if you are dealing with people you do not know well. This is a key week for setting new goals. Putting an end to a problem that has been hanging fire for a long time is likely to get you off to a flying start on something new.

Be prepared for changes in your regular routine. The arrival of unexpected visitors over the weekend could turn out to be a blessing in disguise if you are welcoming and hospitable. New contacts can be made on the work front and also socially. Single Scorpios who are keen to meet a new partner are likely to find fulfillment. More attention to loved ones is emotionally rewarding.

If you are finding it difficult to make ends meet financially, an opportunity that comes up this week could put an end to that situation, at least for the time being. There are also likely to be opportunities to improve your long-term finances. A business deal that has been pending can come to a successful conclusion.

9th Week/February 26–March 4

Thursday the 26th. You are likely to be in for a light-hearted day, both at work and socially. It should not be too difficult to get on with routine matters, since a good mood prevails in just about every quarter. This is a favorable day for making future plans and expanding your horizons. Your vision should be wider than usual, with fewer limitations, either real or imagined, holding you back.

Friday the 27th. Make the most of social activities that come your way today. An invitation to a gathering could put you in touch with a network of people in the know. Make sure they are aware that you are open to new ideas to advance your career. If you are asked to lead a group effort, jump at the chance. It can only enhance your standing.

Saturday the 28th. One of your most deeply desired wishes has a chance of coming true now if you act without hesitation. A different approach to a partner can fulfill your dream. Someone in your social circle has productive ideas. Listen carefully. You can pick up some useful tips. Clear up neglected paperwork. It seems to be piling up.

Sunday March 1st. Try to avoid dealing with complex, detailed work today if you can. Your concentration is likely to be limited. Perhaps you need more time to simply dream and scheme. Expect interruptions to your plans with visits and telephone calls from friends who wish to be in touch. Be flexible and make time for everyone. Your openness will be appreciated.

Monday the 2nd. Domestic life is likely to present some problems. It is probably nothing you cannot handle, but do it promptly. Your closest relationships, including a romance, appear to be a source of greater pleasure. A new involvement should be going from strength to strength. Where property matters are concerned, expect a change of arrangements.

Tuesday the 3rd. Personal relationships continue to be a source of pleasure. Harmony abounds in romance. It appears that you and your partner have found a truer understanding of each other. It is likely that with your help, family members have settled any differences. If you can bridge a communications gap, an old friendship can be renewed. Expect a loved one to make a surprising gesture.

Wednesday the 4th. Focus on important professional goals today. Ambitious Scorpio always wants to achieve. Be wary, however, of pushing too hard. Others want encouragement, not control. Take care of outstanding details in a possible business deal. You may have been concentrating too much on the overall picture. Refrain from extending your credit now. This is the time for pay as you go.

Weekly Summary

This is likely to be a positive and fulfilling week. Focusing more on dreams and special schemes can advance key plans for the future. Let your imagination run away with you, and ideas will come easily. Setting your mind to it can clear away routine tasks easily. Take the opportunity to concentrate on major professional concerns.

You could find introductions to new people important to your future. Friends, allies, or business contacts may come as a result of social networking. If you are new in your neighborhood, invitations are an opportunity to become involved in community affairs. Getting to know neighbors can be of benefit in the future. The weekend appears to find you and your partner closer together.

The week could find you hosting a social gathering that mixes pleasure with business. The result can be the conclusion of a profitable deal. Personal or household finances appear to be stable. Keep them that way by careful spending. Cooperation and harmony are in abundance on the domestic front as family members work together.

10th Week/March 5–11

Thursday the 5th. If somebody owes you a favor, this could be the time when it is returned. The balancing of accounts can improve business affairs. Job efforts you have been putting in lately are likely to begin paying off. Keep up the good work. This is not a time for sitting on your laurels. A social situation that has made you anxious is likely to improve.

Friday the 6th. Long-distance travel is highlighted. Try not to crowd too much else into your day, or you will be rushing. If you are planning a future trip abroad, take time to think about the kinds of currency you will need. Routine jobs may have to be set aside. Don't be reluctant to ask someone to take on extra duties to help you out.

Saturday the 7th. Scorpio with children could find this an ideal time for taking them out for a treat. You are bound to enjoy yourself just as much as they do. For Scorpio without family obligations, this is an ideal time for a change of scene. Be aventurous and go someplace that you have always been meaning to visit. Ask a loved one to accompany you.

Sunday the 8th. Try to be patient today. You may not finish all tasks, but focus on the major ones and get them out of the way. Discussions with family or friends may concern a major change or move. Disagreements could arise to frustrate you. Confrontations are not the answer. If you talk them out, a consensus is likely to be reached.

Monday the 9th. You are still restless, especially where work and career progress are concerned. Someone of influence may be able to give you guidance. His or her support and advice can point the route to success for you. Negotiations in a joint venture remain important. It is likely that others need more time to think. The more reassurance you can offer, the better.

Tuesday the 10th. If you need approval from a higher-up in order to progress with plans you have in mind, this should be a favorable day for seeking it. Spend more time on planning and organizing. It is important that you create a firm base to work from. It could be a while until you start to see results from your efforts. Keep in mind that patience is a virtue.

Wednesday the 11th. It is best to avoid either borrowing from or lending to friends or acquaintances. Doing so could very well complicate your relationships in the future. Be suspicious of someone making overly generous overtures. It is quite possible that he or she is actually after something from you and has dubious motives. Accept a partner's invitation for a social evening.

Weekly Summary

A busy and lively week awaits you. You are likely to be on the move this week, traveling to new and possibly distant places. It is a good idea to keep your schedule flexible, rather than jam packed, especially since in traveling you can encounter unexpected delays. Be prepared to shelve some of your more routine tasks temporarily.

The weekend is an ideal time for getting away from it all by enjoying an outing. If children are involved, perhaps treat them to a special entertainment. A theme park could be the ideal source of enjoyment for everyone concerned. Also put some time aside for older family members who may be counting on your putting in an appearance. This is especially important if some family members do not get out very often to see other people.

Patience and tact are needed where professional matters are concerned. After the weekend you may need to put in more effort to get a backlog of work cleared up. Business negotiations are likely to take more time to conclude than you expect. It is crucial not to rush potential clients or new partners, however. Others may need to have more details from you.

11th Week/March 12–18

Thursday the 12th. Someone of the opposite sex seems to be plaguing you with unwanted attentions. If this person is an acquaintance or friend, you could find it difficult to speak your mind. It is wiser to nip such a tricky situation in the bud. Try to at least bring the matter into the open and have a frank discussion. Do not let embarrassment deter you.

Friday the 13th. A personal problem that has been on your mind seems to be heading for a resolution. Putting difficulties behind you will enable you to move ahead with a more positive attitude. Relaxing and having a chance to think is also bound to lift your spirits. Those around you will understand your desire to be alone.

Saturday the 14th. Efforts today to include loved ones in your plans will pay off. Some past dissension could be resolved, and you can bask in a harmonious environment. A joint venture requires some attention to details. Do not put off getting down to business. Problems of an older person can cause you concern. Your support will be welcome.

Sunday the 15th. You may not feel too sure about the right course of action early in the day. Be patient. One situation appears ready to resolve itself. Signals from those around you also tend to become clear as the day goes on. Take advantage of a surge of creativity. Consider a special interest you have been wanting to pursue purely for pleasure.

Monday the 16th. Play your cards close to the chest today, particularly where business deals are concerned. Others involved are probably doing the same, and it is not to your benefit to push too aggressively for information. Scorpio can be determined and demanding. If you are too rigid now, it could work against you.

Tuesday the 17th. A serious attitude toward work and responsibilities is important today. Try not to worry too much about a course of action to take, however. Others tend to be unpredictable at the moment. You may need to wait until they are more sure of their own plans. Ignore any offhand comments made by those close to you. Striking back can only lead to confrontation.

Wednesday the 18th. Making decisions about choices confronting you appears to be easy now. Knowing more about the attitudes and motives of others has put things in perspective. A piece in a puzzle can now be locked into place. Concentrate on gathering your reserves to fulfill a specific personal goal. Consider beginning a new hobby.

Weekly Summary

Where business or financial matters are concerned, you do best by avoiding direct tactics. Scorpio is secretive by nature. You should have no problem keeping plans to yourself until the moment is right.

Personal problems that have been causing anxiety appear to be resolved this week. You will, however, probably have to take a fairly active role in straightening them out. It is likely that a person whose attentions you are not sure you want to encourage could present a dilemma. Whatever choice you make, keep in mind that your decision could bring a permanent change in your life.

Progress on the work front could be slower than you expected. An unexpected hitch in a project means you have to rely on others to take more responsibility. If they hang back, it will be harder for you to plan your schedule. Be flexible, however. If there is no way out for now, move forward on other work.

12th Week/March 19–25

Thursday the 19th. Avoid being carried away with spending on social activities. Acquaintances or friends are likely to try and persuade you, and you can be tempted to join them. Don't be shy about asking for financial help from family members if you get caught in a difficult situation. It would not be wise to give in to unreasonable demands on the part of someone close to you.

Friday the 20th. Recent career efforts are likely to come together today and bear fruit. Nevertheless, it is a time to keep pressing forward. If you need more money, ask a boss about the possibility of taking on extra work or working longer hours, if this could help. If you have been temporarily out of work, renew your efforts to find another job today.

Saturday the 21st. Be prepared to go with the flow today. Spontaneous invitations are likely to come your way. Planned social activities also are likely go well. Consider treating children to a day out somewhere special. A theme park could be the ideal atmosphere. A change of scene could also be just the ticket to revive tired Scorpio adults.

Sunday the 22nd. Watch out for carelessness where travel plans or social arrangements are concerned. If you have not firmed up plans, now is the time to do so. Good communication appears to be your key to success. A family member may seem a little down. Offer a shoulder to lean on. You can be surprised at how your support will help.

Monday the 23rd. Make an effort to get neglected tasks out of the way today, especially on the job. If you are job hunting, consider covering old ground in your search. Check over your resume. Chances are you can find areas of expertise you could promote. This can be a productive day if you listen to the advice of someone in the know.

Tuesday the 24th. This looks like a very favorable day for Scorpio involved in financial or property negotiations. You are at a point where an exchange of contracts may well take place. Be sure to read all the small print. A family member could call upon you to help resolve a personal problem. Give your support, but avoid taking sides.

Wednesday the 25th. If you are hoping to begin a new project, hobby, or venture today, you may have to be patient. It is likely that the backing you need will be temporarily held up. Try to focus your attention on an area where you will be able to make some progress right away. Aim not to take any disappointment out on loved ones, especially a romantic partner.

Weekly Summary

Both personal and business funds need to be handled with care this week. You can be tempted to go over-board in a social situation, especially when others are very persuasive. Think carefully before taking the plunge. If you find yourself without funds for a bill that is pressing, someone close to you can probably lend a temporary hand. The week is favorable if you are involved in real estate deals. It is likely that negotiations can be concluded to your benefit.

Work efforts made in the past could pay off this week. But this is not the time to slack off. It appears there is plenty still to do. In fact, Scorpio struggling with personal or family finances could probably benefit from seeking new earning possibilities. If you can take on more duties at work, you can reap future benefits.

The social scene appears to be lively and energetic. Opt for a change of scene on the weekend. Choose places suitable for the entire family so that everyone can enjoy a break. Plan your time well. If you are going a distance, travel could present some problems. Romance can take a delightful turn if you put your best foot forward. Someone else probably expects you to make a gesture.

13th Week/March 26–April 1

Thursday the 26th. Mix business with pleasure and make this a profitable day. If you regularly participate in a sport, you are likely to do very well now. Luck seems to be on the side of Scorpio who is entering competitions and tournaments. If you are involved in a new romance, you can deepen the relationship now by spending more time together. Think of others first today.

Friday the 27th. Your professional life appears to be moving into high gear. It appears that a promotion is more on your mind than usual. A boss is likely to be keeping a benevolent eye on you. If you make your goals known, he or she will probably make efforts to support you. Aim to establish a new and more productive routine if you are self-employed.

Saturday the 28th. Try to get burdensome tasks out of the way early on in the day. You should be able to make some excellent progress. This looks like a propitious time for social gatherings in your home. Ask family members to get involved in the preparations. You will not have too much to do on your own and others will be eager to cooperate.

Sunday the 29th. Financial concerns may encourage you to put rest aside and do some work instead. Be prepared for quite a busy day, no matter what you decide to do. More than one opportunity to alleviate a tricky romantic situation is likely to come your way. Try not to judge your loved one too harshly. Whatever he or she has done was probably thoughtless but not intentional.

Monday the 30th. Close relationships should be back on an even keel today. Your mate or spouse is likely to be acting a little out of the ordinary, but in your favor. A lovely gift could come your way. If you are feeling romantic, show it. You are likely to receive a warm response. Try to be supportive if your partner is worried about the unknown.

Tuesday the 31st. Key developments are likely to take place today where business negotiations are concerned. Others seem to have made compromises. Be prepared to put your pen to paper and sign a contract. You should only do so, however, if you feel absolutely satisfied with the agreement. Unsure Scorpio is advised to wait a little longer and reconsider the situation.

Wednesday April 1st. It is best to avoid combining business with pleasure today. Others who are in a party mood may not be able to carry out commitments they make now. Allowing a friend to give you personal advice may not be to your advantage. Consider your previous experience. There could be an ulterior motive.

Weekly Summary

You appear to be going through a lucky phase this week. If you do not normally enter competitions because you think you never win, think again. It might be worth your while to take a chance. You have nothing to lose, and you might have something to gain. Financial and business concerns take up time now. Discussions and negotiations will go well if you pay attention to details. Expect others to come around to your way of thinking.

Professional aims and ambitions are likely to be important this week. This is a good time to try and move ahead, since people in high places have an eye on you and will most likely support and help you. Entertaining business associates you do not know well at home can be a good way to break the ice and encourage more cordial relations.

Gifts, bonuses, and extra earning opportunities are

all likely to come your way this week. Make sure that you put some time aside to enjoy your social life, as well as trying to improve the family finances. Your partner may need your support more than usual. If you are single, Monday is likely to be a key time for making new personal contacts.

14th Week/April 2–8

Thursday the 2nd. Long-distance travel is highlighted today. If you are taking a trip for professional purposes, be prepared with all the paperwork you need. You could be called upon to make a presentation. Dress for the occasion. A trip for personal reasons could find you meeting with a surprise. Someone you had not expected to see could bring back memories.

Friday the 3rd. Broadening your social life is a key theme today. You will probably have the opportunity to expand your circle of friends. Be open to invitations, especially if they involve those in your profession. Focus on using spare time for a cultural activity. Visiting an art gallery or a museum is bound to be stimulating. You might consider that play you have been wanting to see.

Saturday the 4th. Do not try to do two things at once now. You cannot be in more than one place at a time. Put your priorities in order and make your choice. You may not be feeling up to par physically. This is probably the time to shed some old habits and begin a new health regimen. You might persuade others to follow your example.

Sunday the 5th. A business scheme is likely to be tempting because it involves making a lot of money in a short period of time. But does it really? Look into the matter further. The whole situation may be a lot more complicated and difficult than it appears at first. Talks with people who are older and probably wiser should be useful.

Monday the 6th. This ought to be a fairly trouble-free day. Whatever you set out to do, you will most likely achieve your goals with a great deal of ease. Make hay while the sun shines. Seldom do you have such a time when obstacles are out of the way and you can make easy progress. Discussions with someone of influence are likely to be eye-opening.

Tuesday the 7th. One of your friendships could be about to move into a more complicated phase. The person in question may start to make romantic overtures. These could be quite out of the blue as far as you are concerned. If you are not happy with the new developments, say something. Diplomacy is helpful. Do not just stick your head in the sand.

Wednesday the 8th. The time may be right for taking a professional step forward. Someone you do not expect to can give you a helping hand. A community event could put you in a leadership role. Grasp the opportunity to be creative and let others know about your special talents. A communication from a distance brings welcome news.

Weekly Summary

This is a week for working on broadening your horizons. Travel to faraway places may beckon. If you do not have time to take a break at the moment, you might get some vacation brochures together and plan a trip for the future. If you are traveling in connection with work, take your time to prepare properly for a long journey.

Scorpio's social life is likely to open up more as the week progresses. Accept various invitations, especially if they mean that you will come into contact with different people. New friends and acquaintances can be made in several areas of your life. If you have recently changed jobs, new people around you are likely to be friendly and hospitable. This is probably going to be a key week for establishing deeper contacts and relationships all around.

Be suspicious about a business proposition that appears too good to be true. It is likely that you will be able to make some sound, overall work progress after the weekend. An opportunity to chat more generally with someone higher up could bring some interesting and useful information to light.

15th Week/April 9–15

Thursday the 9th. This will probably be a more carefree day than usual. Recent domestic problems seem to have resolved themselves. A possible unexpected windfall can allow you to splurge a bit on yourself. You could be thinking your appearance needs some improvement. Do not feel guilty if you indulge yourself.

Friday the 10th. If you are preparing for the Passover or Easter holiday, you could be kept busy. You can probably get more done if you take on major tasks yourself. Delegate details to others. Avoid distractions or interruptions. This is not the time to become irritated by the demands of those around you.

Saturday the 11th. Visitors you had not been counting on could disrupt your schedule. Since you probably got major chores out of the way earlier, you can afford to be welcoming. Younger family members may need some special attention today. Try to find the time to accommodate them. Their joy will be your reward.

Sunday the 12th. However you celebrate this Easter holiday, you are bound to find others congenial. Playing host today can bring out your charm and generosity. If there is someone who could use your company and help, make time for him or her. Making visits or taking a short trip can be easier than you expect.

Monday the 13th. It is possible that your self-esteem is looking for a boost today. It is best not to rely on others to give you the confidence you feel you need. Colleagues or loved ones appear to be concerned with their own problems. Try something you like to do. Exercise in the outdoors might do wonders for you.

Tuesday the 14th. This should be a much less troublesome day than yesterday. Much of your confidence is likely to be returning. You would be wise to keep out of the way of other people's troubles, however. You could end up being dragged into a very tiresome situation otherwise. You need not lack sympathy. Simply do not get too involved.

Wednesday the 15th. Watch your finances today. Overspending is possible, especially if you are feeling blue. Friends or family are unlikely to be of much help. Scorpio has a natural inner strength and determination. Draw on this to help you to say no to something that you know will simply not be to your benefit.

Weekly Summary

You will probably do your best work this week when you have a quiet environment to work in. However, emotional issues can play havoc with your concentration. If you are leery of contact with someone whose motives you are unsure of, it might be wise to make the first move. Do not avoid dealing with any situation that is giving you grief. The sooner you find a way to handle it, the better.

Avoid going to extremes of any kind. It is best to find a balance between work and rest this week. Although you may wish to get a lot done, you probably will not be doing anyone any favors if you push yourself too hard. Make a point of taking regular breaks so that you have a chance to rest and recuperate. A change of scene will give you a boost physically and mentally.

Stresses and strains could take their toll this week. You are likely to wish you could be free from domestic and job pressures. Take time to look after your physical and mental well-being. You can find that even mild exercise, like a brisk walk to get away from it all, will revive your spirits and renew self-confidence.

16th Week/April 16–22

Thursday the 16th. The same issues involving money that were of concern yesterday seem to prevail today. If you know that shopping will tempt you to spend more than you should, try to avoid it. If you want to show a loved one how much you care, find another way than an expensive present. Use your imagination to give pleasure to your partner.

Friday the 17th. Make a point of being more in touch with those around you. This is a favorable day for catching up on your correspondence. Balance your financial books also. Contacts from the past could be helpful in aiding you to get a new business venture off the ground. You may find that a neighbor or acquaintance has some advice you could use.

Saturday the 18th. Information from someone distant could give you an insight into a perplexing personal problem. You can press ahead now to resolve the situation. Let family or friends know you are open to social activities. Someone is bound to come up with ideas that will arouse your curiosity. Married Scorpio can find children especially enjoyable today.

Sunday the 19th. If you are planning a trip, make sure all arrangements are in place. It might be wise to remind others who may be involved of the plans. This is not a good day to listen to gossip or to pass it on. Keep whatever you hear to yourself. Avoid the temptation to jump to conclusions, since you are likely to be hearing only one side of the story.

Monday the 20th. Expect the unexpected where other people's behavior is concerned. Home life in particular can be up and down because those around you are not happy. It is important that you do not take others' moodiness too personally. This is a favorable day for more restless Scorpio who is searching for a change of pace.

Tuesday the 21st. It appears that you need to establish some order around you today. Set some priorities for domestic or work chores and get to them. Let those around you know that you mean business. If trips are involved, organize a schedule and stick to it. You have the ability to inspire others to cooperate. If you want to relax with a social evening, you need not feel guilty.

Wednesday the 22nd. Romance is in the air for Scorpio today. If you are unattached, this could be the right moment to meet the partner of your dreams. A social event could provide the opportunity. If you are already involved, give your relationship a boost. Let your loved one know that you have a very romantic side.

Weekly Summary

It is probably necessary to cut back more on spending this week. Scorpio can sometimes feel more of a need to spend when you do not have the money for it! Try to keep occupied with other matters so that you are not tempted to go out on a mad shopping spree. Where new business matters are concerned and new work is sought, look to various current and past contacts for help.

Your social scene should be lively, but you may have to work at it. This is a good week for getting back in touch with people you have not seen or heard from in a while. It would be wise to be organized when making social or travel arrangements. Confirm schedules, and make sure others are aware of your plans.

Home life seems prone to some change or disruptions. Much of the problem has to do with those around you who are sending mixed signals. If you see that someone is perplexed, try to do all you can to help. Not only will it cheer the person up, but it will probably make the overall atmosphere a lot more pleasant for you all. Romantic involvements this week appear to be all that Scorpio could wish for.

17th Week/April 23–29

Thursday the 23rd. It appears you are making good progress on the job front. Colleagues and superiors are aware of your efforts. It is likely that a team effort is required to complete a project. Do not hesitate if you are asked to take a leadership role. Self-employed Scorpio could benefit from new contacts.

Friday the 24th. A joint venture is likely to prove fruitful if you listen to professional advice. You do not have all the answers yet. Someone more objective can be of immense help. Unless you consider a loved one's point of view, a romance could be in jeopardy. Understanding is the key to restoring harmony.

Saturday the 25th. By nature, Scorpio tends to be quite intense. It appears you are taking yourself a little too seriously now. Avoid trying to excercise personal authority. Others are not likely to take kindly to your being the boss in every situation. You probably need to step back and relax. Determine to take things in stride and give others some space.

Sunday the 26th. Social activities could improve your spirits today. If a community or neighborhood event is being held, try to attend. Meeting others outside your circle could put you in a more cheerful mood. If you have put aside an interesting project, consider taking it up again. You could get some new ideas.

Monday the 27th. Personal relationships are likely to improve if you are willing to put aside petty issues. Determine to restore harmony by compromising. Someone older may need your support now. If some change is involved, sit down and talk it over. You could have to take charge and make plans on the person's behalf.

Tuesday the 28th. Be careful about overspending today. This is also a day for taking a cautious attitude where investments are concerned. An opportunity that looks appealing could turn out to be quite suspicious when you investigate it further. If you are already taking part in a business plan, make every effort to find out the exact position of others involved.

Wednesday the 29th. If this is a rough period for personal finances, consider getting some extra work. You could have good luck in contacting former colleagues who know of employment opportunities. It is possible you need to exercise more willpower in your spending. It would be wise to make up a budget and stick to it.

Weekly Summary

Career opportunities are strongly highlighted in the first part of the week. This is an especially favorable time for Scorpio to make beneficial contacts with influential people. Superiors appear to be very aware of your efforts. Their support is essential. A leadership role could come your way, and you are bound to make the most of it. Self-employed Scorpio is likely to find projects when the right contacts are made.

Close relationships need more careful handling. Scorpio seems to be more demanding now. It is likely that you will have to compromise with a partner's desires to some extent if you are to keep the peace. The more you are prepared to give in your relationships, the better they are likely to be just now.

Be wary of making investments on impulse. It is advisable to do some background research and seek professional advice. Look to your long-term security where money is concerned. For the time being, you could help the situation by taking on extra work or by building up a private business interest.

18th Week/April 30–May 6

Thursday the 30th. A change of scene is likely to do you a world of good. A business trip may be the answer. Or you could be at a meeting or conference in a new setting. Even changing your daily routine can give you a lift. Look for a new kind of entertainment or activity to enjoy with a friend or loved one.

Friday May 1st. Spring weather arouses spring fever. If you are feeling restless, get going on some vacation plans. A trip to a distant place is probably appealing. To fulfill your dreams, be realistic and put budget priorities in order. Begin saving now, rather than rely on credit cards. A fine romance is just ahead.

Saturday the 2nd. Support from others is likely to come only after an initial disagreement. Scorpio is not generally in the habit of voicing his or her troubles. If you want help with solving a problem, however, do not expect other people to be mind readers. Make an effort to explain your position and your intentions so that others can come to your aid.

Sunday the 3rd. Much-needed support seems hard to come by at the moment. Perhaps this is because you are looking in the wrong place. A loved one probably has enough of his or her own problems to contend with just now. A conversation with a stranger could turn out to be surprisingly helpful. Try not to neglect practical tasks that need attention around the home.

Monday the 4th. This is likely to be a productive day. The conclusion of a business deal appears imminent, but you may have to travel to finalize the arrangements. A colleague in the know probably has information you could use to your advantage. Make it a point to meet with him or her. Listen carefully and benefit.

Tuesday the 5th. Look to friends for help and support today. Somebody that your partner knows could turn out to be a very useful contact. You could be meeting new people. Do not be too quick to draw conclusions about them. If you are being accepted by people who do not know you well, it is to your advantage to treat them the same way.

Wednesday the 6th. People you have recently come into contact with are likely to offer social invitations. This is an excellent time for developing these relationships. Pursue new interests as well. You seem to want to spread your wings more. Keep an eye on spending. All this exciting new activity could end up burning a hole in your pocket.

Weekly Summary

New and different surroundings are bound to perk up your spirits and possibly change some of your ideas this week. You are not likely to be stuck in a rut. You will probably shift some of your views and see life from a different perscpective. If you do, you can find that some problems are not as serious as you thought.

Some strain is possible in your relationships with others, either on the job or at home. You will probably realize that much of this stems from your inability to express your true feelings. Scorpio is not generally shy about speaking up. So let others know what bothers you. The sooner you do, the sooner you can get the support you need and want.

Your career prospects look promising. Make the most of an opportunity to get on good terms with an influential person who may be able to help you. It is also possible this week to get to know some social acquaintances much better. A deepening of your relationships is likely to make it easier to find emotional support when you need it in the future.

19th Week/May 7–13

Thursday the 7th. It appears that you are in need of a rest today. Any overindulgences on the social scene are likely to have caught up with you. Keeping your diet simple will help you recuperate. Activities in the fresh air can also revive you. It would probably be best to keep to yourself until you feel better. You might not be good company.

Friday the 8th. It appears you will have more time to yourself at work today. Use the opportunity to chart your own schedule. Try to press ahead with the tasks that interest you personally. You are likely to make good progress. Make a point of clearing away routine jobs first though, especially if they have been piling up on you.

Saturday the 9th. Look forward to a busy day, with household chores taking priority. You probably will need some help from others. Make your case and ask them to share in the duties. Their response is likely to please you. If renovations are in order, make sure you have all the materials and equipment you need.

Sunday the 10th. This is likely to be a day full of surprises. Time to yourself will probably be hard to find. Family members or friends appear to have specific ideas about how you will spend your time. If you choose to go your own way, you could meet with some uncomfortable disapproval. Determine to do what you feel is right for you now.

Monday the 11th. Scorpio is naturally a person of determination. This is even more apparent today. If you wish to pursue a creative interest, do so. You are likely to get very encouraging results. If you are feeling bored, consider developing a new interest or hobby. A return to an old pastime could also be rewarding.

Tuesday the 12th. This is a favorable day for Scorpio eager to be on the move. Start looking for property to buy or rent or lease. What you want is likely to come your way today. Check your financial situation. The overall picture should be much better. If there is still room for improvement, think about new ways of increasing your income.

Wednesday the 13th. A lack of funding is likely to get in the way of moving forward with a joint venture. This does not have to stop the project entirely. If your assets are in order, consider a loan. It would not be wise, however, to borrow from family or friends. Such obligations could put you in an awkward position.

Weekly Summary

It is wise to slow down the pace this week, especially if you have been burning the candle at both ends. Paying more attention to your well-being is bound to be beneficial. Look for ways to change some of your eating habits. You might set aside time in the evenings to exercise, preferably in the outdoors. And avoid overindulging in a social whirl.

Professionally, there are likely to be opportunities to take on more responsibility. Bosses seem eager to entrust you with a number of projects or tasks in their absence. Your artistic and creative talents could come to the fore. You appear to have an idea about turning a special interest into a lucrative endeavor.

Money matters should be relatively stable. If you are hoping to complete real estate negotiations, a favorable deal seems likely after the weekend. Other projects could require additional funding. Borrowing money may be the answer, but look around carefully to get the best bargain.

20th Week/May 14–20

Thursday the 14th. The tricky situation you seem to have been going through where money is concerned continues today. Nevertheless, there is likely to be a golden opportunity to improve your overall position. And it does not necessarily have to mean sacrificing a great deal of time or giving up social opportunities. Keep your ears open and your eyes peeled.

Friday the 15th. It is advisable to hold your tongue today when you are in the company of bosses or colleagues. Much as you may be irritated at another person's words or deeds, it is not a good idea to create a dispute. If you are thinking of a career move, this is a favorable day for following your intuition. You should have a lot to gain by doing so.

Saturday the 16th. It could do you good to break up your routine today. Visits to relatives or neighbors can be a rewarding experience. Children can be especially fun today. Think about organizing an activity with youngsters or taking a jaunt to someplace different. An introduction to someone new could spark up the life of single Scorpio.

Sunday the 17th. Put aside some time to make plans for the future. If you are considering a move or major change, it is important to sort out your exact priorities and requirements. Balance your personal books today. If accounts need paying off, try to get caught up with the situation. A family gathering is likely to be more pleasurable than you might expect.

Monday the 18th. Today could be significant in bringing business discussions to a close. It appears you have a chance to win an important client or conclude a contract. The key to your success is reassuring those involved that their interests are taken care of. A difficult person could turn out to be an ally.

Tuesday the 19th. It is a good idea at the moment to bear in mind that certain aspects of your life are probably quite transitory. Someone you enjoy being with may need to move on soon. You can have fun together, but it would not be wise to invest too much emotionally in this relationship, especially if it is a romantic one. Be realistic and save yourself a lot of hurt.

Wednesday the 20th. You are likely to have an enjoyable and rewarding day. Make the most of creative urges and get involved in a hobby or other pleasurable interest. It is quite possible that you can turn such endeavor into a business enterprise. Consider involving some who think like you do. It is worth talking to a person you feel may be able to help.

Weekly Summary

Tact and diplomacy are likely to be a major factor in your career and business life. You may have a tendency to be outspoken in your opposition to the opinions of others. This is not the time to speak out too vehemently. You can gain clients or important contracts by letting others know you are flexible.

Social activities this week are likely to break up your routine. Others will be pleased to enjoy your company. Use part of the weekend to pay attention to children. Activities with young ones bring their own special rewards. Romance does not seem to be neglected, either.

Be open to someone new, especially if you are on the rebound.

Your own creative talents can make this a favorable week for turning around any problems with funds. An artistic enterprise can gain the attention of someone whose help you can probably use. Don't hesitate to discuss your ideas. You could find an enthusiastic supporter.

21st Week/May 21–27

Thursday the 21st. Take time today to sort and clear out your cabinets, closets, and desk. Files, documents, clothing, and all sorts of paperwork have probably been piling up. Getting organized is bound to make work easier. Avoid the temptation to hang on to things you do not need. You might donate them to a worthwhile cause.

Friday the 22nd. A long weekend is coming up, and you want to be prepared. Be aware that delays and foul-ups could occur if you are traveling. Firm up plans right away. If tasks at work are taking longer than expected, ask a colleague for help. Someone who has little to do could be happy to relieve the boredom.

Saturday the 23rd. Spend a lot of time with your loved one today. He or she may be feeling neglected. Discuss plans for your future together. Resolve to settle recent disagreements or conflicts that may have upset you both. A loving and compassionate approach is sure to bring you closer together.

Sunday the 24th. If today includes visits or a short trip, make sure you will be welcome. Unexpected visits are sometimes fun, but not always. If your plans include a celebration with friends or family, it is best to make it a quiet one. Recent events indicate you are not in the mood for expensive entertaining.

Monday the 25th. The last day of the Memorial Day weekend is probably a time to relax. You can think about work pressures tomorrow. Seek out enjoyable company. A possible social event may not be very appealing. If you feel you must attend, make an appearance and leave as soon as you can.

Tuesday the 26th. Aim to keep a balanced perspective today. In your determination to succeed, you could overreach yourself. A more conciliatory approach to others is called for if you want to persuade them to accept your views. Especially be cautious in financial or business negotiations. Loosen up and relax more.

Wednesday the 27th. Many past cares appear to roll away now since domestic harmony has been restored. Keep yourself on an even keel, and the week will be smooth sailing. Responsibilities on the job appear to be unevenly distributed. It is not to your advantage to be silent. Let others know you are concerned and want the situation corrected.

Weekly Summary

This is an excellent week for clearing out some of the deadwood in your life. Scorpio is efficient and does not like clutter. You are undoubtedly ready to part with items no longer needed. Neglected paperwork also needs organizing and sorting if you want to have a sense of accomplishment. You might think about developing a new personal image as well. Feel good with a new wardrobe or hairstyle.

A more fulfilling relationship with your loved one highlights your week. It appears that more understanding and consideration have inspired a stronger bond. Plan now for your future together. You are probably looking forward to a long-term commitment.

Aim to gain the cooperation and support of your co-workers. Schedules could be bungled and projects delayed because of the work load. If you feel others are not pulling their weight, do not hesitate to speak up. Superiors may need some prodding, but exercise tact, and you will accomplish your goal.

22nd Week/May 28–June 3

Thursday the 28th. Be wary of taking on major responsibilities today. Emotional problems that have been diverting your attention are likely to intrude into your thoughts. Confront your anxieties, and make every attempt to overcome them. You need your time to deal with some pressing job matters. Determine to meet commitments you have made.

Friday the 29th. Pressure on the job can disrupt your concentration today. Interruptions by others can distract you from the work at hand. Rather than endure the stress, try to get away. Find a quiet place. Being alone can encourage a different perspective on the situation. Make sure, however, that you are not just running away from a problem.

Saturday the 30th. It is likely that you will be able to clear up an old problem once and for all now. This is a favorable day for coming to grips with new ventures. Start doing some major planning. Look to people who have had more experience. They will be a great help if you make your situation clear. Attend to any neglected domestic responsibilities.

Sunday the 31st. Work on fulfilling a strongly held wish or desire today. There is a good chance you will accomplish your goal. At least you can start moving in the right direction. It is important to choose the right people to help you with a new project. Select carefully. Someone who appears to be committed to your interests may be covering something up.

Monday June 1st. A friendship that has so far been quite warm may come under pressure today. You could end up arguing over money matters. Try to keep things in perspective. If there is depth to your relationship, trivial matters are not likely to wreck it completely. You both probably have to decide whether the contentious issue is indeed only trivial or more serious.

Tuesday the 2nd. Someone with whom you seldom see eye-to-eye is likely to be particularly irritating. Nip the situation in the bud before you are pushed too far. A confrontation now is not in your best interests. Scorpio has a tendency occasionally to dramatize. You do not want to regret your actions later.

Wednesday the 3rd. Privacy is always important to you and especially so today. Keep any domestic problems within the family circle. Strangers may occasionally be good listeners. They can also spread your secrets. If you feel you must confide in someone, choose a dear friend whom you know you can trust and who will give you support.

Weekly Summary

Emotional ups and downs are likely to throw you a bit off course this week. It is of little benefit to ponder problems whose solutions are not immediately obvious. Focus your energies on those situations you can do something about now. Where loved ones are concerned, you could be drawn into disputes that are not your responsibility to solve. Let those involved handle it.

A change of scene may be called for if pressures on the job front seem insurmountable. You need not travel far to be alone for a time to get your thoughts in perspective. Those who may be trying to push you into hasty actions should be avoided. You will have to back off to assess the situation before you do or say something you will later regret.

Issues over money could be worrisome this week. Take care that a relationship is not ruptured because money is involved. A longtime friendship is worth more than dollars. A new financial venture appears promising. But it demands close attention and some investigation of others involved.

23rd Week/June 4–10

Thursday the 4th. Do all you can to complete a business or real estate deal. Luck appears to be on your side. It is probably worth putting out feelers by making an initial offer. If others are involved in the venture, get their input. Do make sure, however, that funding is available before you make your move.

Friday the 5th. Travel for business or professional reasons is indicated today. Get all preparations in order to avoid any frustrations on the road. For some, a romance appears to be on a collision course. Do not be stubborn about letting go. It is most likely your pride rather than your heart that is hurt.

Saturday the 6th. You should be able to make marked progress toward fulfilling personal goals today. Research or studies you may have been working on could be completed. Someone probably has some ideas about a creative venture you are involved in. Let him or her advise you on the best course to follow.

Sunday the 7th. You may be prevented from accomplishing some practical tasks by concern over a loved one. A mate or partner seems to be feeling insecure. It is important that you give of your time. Put aside your plans and give him or her your wholehearted attention. Your love will blossom anew.

Monday the 8th. Avoid combining business with pleasure, especially if new clients or new employers are involved. It is wiser to get to know them better before you entertain them. If you want to socialize, plan a party with friends. Or start organizing an outing. Sports activities could have an appeal.

Tuesday the 9th. This should be a productive day for Scorpio hoping to be on the move soon. Concentrate on places where you think you would like to live, and begin looking. Should you find something that interests you, consider making an offer. A deal is likely to take shape. Be wary, however, of incentives that may not be all they seem.

Wednesday the 10th. It is probably a good idea to check your budget today. You appear to be coping with a temporary lack of sufficient funds. If a loved one has been a bit loose with money, this could become a bone of contention. But be sure to find out just where the money has gone before you start placing blame. You could be at fault yourself.

Weekly Summary

Business transactions are likely to be to your benefit this week. Scorpio's ability to get to the heart of a matter stands you in good stead. You can find that lengthy negotiations are not necessary when you are sure of what you want. Funding need not be a problem if you get the proper backing. Others who may be involved with you can offer good advice. A move may be in the offing. But proceed with caution.

Domestic and romantic situations could intrude into your time this week. The middle of the week appears to be especially sensitive. A loved one needs a great deal of reassurance. If you have been neglectful or lacking in understanding, determine to make up for it. Romance is rocky now. Letting go is difficult, but is probably the wisest course.

If you are in a new job or business situation, hold off on socializing. For now the best course is to focus on work rather than entertainment. Unwise spending by another could put finances in a bind. You too could be at fault. Take a close look at the budget. Belt tightening may be in order.

24th Week/June 11–17

Thursday the 11th. If you are planning a shopping trip, take a good friend or loved one along with you. It is likely that, between you, you will find what you are looking for more easily. Be sure to confer if you are planning to buy items for the home or materials for decorating. Entertainment with those close to you is favored this evening.

Friday the 12th. This is an excellent day for spending time with loved ones. You are likely to be much happier when you are in company of close friends or family. If you are beginning a new project, it should be beneficial to get a loved one involved. Joint business associations are favored today. Start talking to associates in related fields of endeavor.

Saturday the 13th. If you are putting on a special event in your home, get family members in on the act. A garage sale could bring in some much needed cash. This is also a good day for your own home shopping. In fact, you could find some bargains yourself at garage sales. A relative is likely to need some support with an emotional problem. Do all you can to help.

Sunday the 14th. Home life should be harmonious and enjoyable. It is important not to keep secrets from your nearest and dearest. Being silent may create friction between you. Others are more sensitive than you think. They are likely to sense if you are holding something back. Look to your future financial security and make some plans.

Monday the 15th. Major job responsibilities appear to demand attention today. Your efficiency and organizational abilities may have thrust you into a leadership role. Higher-ups are probably looking to you for decisions. Proceed with confidence. Scorpio in a public position has an opportunity to make an impact.

Tuesday the 16th. You can have an influence today on someone you care about. His or her behavior seems to have upset you. Be firm in making your concerns known. Your straightforward approach is likely to help the person gain insight into the problem. Single Scorpio has a chance to make a good impression on someone new.

Wednesday the 17th. Curb any impulses to entertain lavishly. You could be thinking of an at-home party or enjoying an expensive restaurant. You do not have such deep pockets now. There are other ways of trying to impress people. A creative venture may be frustrating you. Drop it for now and resume at a later time.

Weekly Summary

This week looks very positive where close relationships are concerned. Greater intimacy with your partner is likely if you spend more time together. If you are planning to purchase items for the home or for your wardrobe, try to shop with your loved one in tow. There are bargains to be had, but it may take two pairs of eyes to track them down.

Entertaining at home can be successful this week. You are unlikely to have to go far for activities during your leisure time. Be wary of overspending. Others understand your need to watch your pocketbook now. Confide in loved ones about any problems that are on your mind. This is a time for giving and receiving more support in the domestic environment.

Your professional life should be enhanced when you take the initiative. Group efforts are encouraged, with you in a prominent role. When your talents come to the fore, you can be unstoppable. A business or financial situation appears to be stable now. Keep it that way. Do not be tempted to indulge in speculation.

25th Week/June 18–24

Thursday the 18th. Scorpio has a knack for achieving great accomplishments when you are determined and have a goal in mind. Set your sights high professionally. Those with influence are sure to encourage your ambitions. Read the small print before signing any documents. Consult an expert if necessary.

Friday the 19th. This is a day when cooperation with others is essential. Domestic plans could be up in the air unless you consult closely with the family. If travel is involved, make sure everyone is properly prepared.

At work, focus on a major project that requires a group effort. Details could slip through the cracks.

Saturday the 20th. Friction between you and a partner could arise. It is probably a trivial matter that has been blown out of proportion. You both share some blame. You might suggest a truce and a change of scene. Going on an outing or taking a quiet walk together could go a long way toward clearing the air.

Sunday the 21st. It appears that efforts yesterday have restored harmony. Making a point of being understanding and considerate has paid off. Make some long-term plans with your loved one for the future. For some Scorpio, personal reflection on your state of mind may be foremost. You can gain insight by looking inward at your hidden agenda.

Monday the 22nd. Home decoration or refurbishing appears to take up time now. If professionals are involved, you are likely to be pleased with their efforts. Self-employed Scorpio may need to change some work habits. Realize that you can accomplish more if you get organized. Clear your desk and rearrange the work place.

Tuesday the 23rd. This is not a good day to take unnecessary risks. Friends and acquaintances may try to talk you into something you feel unsure about. Trust your own intuition and judgment. Somebody around you looks ready to make a fool of him or herself. His or her mistake could turn out to be quite costly. You probably saw it coming. But try to be sympathetic.

Wednesday the 24th. Try a change of scene today. You will probably get more done in a different environment. Even getting away for a break would be beneficial. It is important not to lose sight of what really matters to you. This should be a useful day for planning for the future, especially if you are temporarily out of work. Think carefully about your goals, and look at new options.

Weekly Summary

Your work scene should be smooth going. This will likely be a good week for catching up on neglected tasks and for fulfilling basic, routine endeavors. For Scorpio who is self-employed, the same applies. In addition, you may benefit from putting an entirely new routine in place. Consider alternative working methods. Organize to speed up your productivity and bring a greater degree of efficiency all around.

Relations with your loved one are likely to present some conflicts. You can get on each other's nerves if you spend too much time cooped up in the home. Try a change of scene instead. Do something together you both enjoy. You will find you both are more able to appreciate your mutual good points. The result will be a greater understanding on both sides.

Financial or business matters could pose some risks if you are not cautious. If you are uncertain about the venture, back away. Generally, funds are not a problem. It might be wise, however, to take a look at your budget. There are probably areas where you could find some savings. Extra money is likely to come in handy.

26th Week/June 25–July 1

Thursday the 25th. A short trip for pleasure could help relieve pressures you may be feeling. If possible, a boat ride or an outing near the water seems appealing. Try to find a congenial companion to join you. Someone new you meet could be a source of inspiration for an interesting project. It need not involve a long-term commitment.

Friday the 26th. Get moving early in the day if you want to catch an employer or boss during a free period. This should be a beneficial day for discussing your career future. Talks could involve a possible pay raise or promotion. Scorpio who needs references would be wise to ask for them now. Putting it off until another time could prove awkward in the end.

Saturday the 27th. Some Scorpios have to forget about relaxing today. Joint financial matters are likely to intrude. A new deal can be struck up. Put your mind to future planning in relation to needed funding. Group efforts are likely to be helpful if you are based at work today. You tend to get a lot more done when responsibilities are shared.

Sunday the 28th. Put neglected personal plans into effect today. If others are not in agreement, go your own way. You need some space for yourself. A friend who intervenes in a situation may have good intentions. His or her intervention probably only confuses the matter, however. Accept an invitation to socialize.

Monday the 29th. This is a day for expecting the unexpected. Be prepared for a complete alteration in your plans. It is best to maintain a flexible stance. Business and financial affairs seem to be prone to more fluctuations than usual. Do not be too quick to judge the situation, however. The results at the end of the day could give you a pleasant surprise.

Tuesday the 30th. A friend appears to be making an effort to forge deeper bonds in your relationship. This may not suit you just at the moment, however. You can tend to be suspicious of other people's motives if they are overly friendly. In this instance, you are probably not simply being paranoid. You would be wise to trust your inner feelings.

Wednesday July 1st. You are likely to get the most done when you are involved in behind-the-scenes activities. Leave the public relations strategies to others for a while. Privacy now will be important in all areas of your life. Scorpio is naturally a private person and can do without other people prying into your personal affairs.

Weekly Summary

A change of scene is likely to be a real tonic for frazzled and tired Scorpio this week. It is best to take yourself off to a different environment. Getting away can renew your vitality and clear your mind. Once you have had a rest from routine and ongoing tasks, you are more likely to make sound progress personally and professionally.

Where your career is concerned, there will probably be a key opportunity this week to discuss your future plans. Take a broader perspective and aim high. If you feel that a promotion or raise is due to you, now is the time to speak up. Make a point of getting preparations under way if you are thinking of changing jobs. This might include contacting bosses or employers so that references can easily be obtained in the future.

It appears that a relationship requires you to tread carefully. You would be wise to keep a distance until you are sure of your feelings. Getting too close too soon could cloud your judgment. Friendship can be less than helpful this week. Others seem to want to jump in where they are not wanted. Let them know you cherish your privacy.

27th Week/July 2–8

Thursday the 2nd. Rest and relaxation are needed more than usual today. It might be a good idea to go for a checkup if you are worried about a persistent condition. It is quite likely that you will feel better once you have caught up on sleep, however. Try to avoid taking on further commitments and responsibilities until you really feel up to them.

Friday the 3rd. It appears you have gotten back on a more even keel now. Possibly the idea of a Fourth of July holiday has perked you up. Plan some celebration with those whose company you enjoy. You could feel like attending festivities. If so, check your neighborhood or community to find out what is being planned.

Saturday the 4th. Long-distance travel may not be easy on this holiday. Congestion and delays could hold you up. Short trips or local visits would most likely be easier. Avoid any temptation to have your own fireworks. There should be plenty of displays for you to enjoy. Try to include children in your activities.

Sunday the 5th. Your creativity appears to be peaking. This is an excellent time for beginning a new hobby or taking up a new interest. Plan some special events. Family or friends are probably just waiting for you to come up with ideas. Your confidence is on the increase. You can trust your judgment more and carve out a clear direction for yourself.

Monday the 6th. If anyone has made a mistake in relation to financial arrangements, they are likely to admit it now. The situation should work out entirely in your favor. Do check all relevant paperwork, however. Some details that are not so easy to spot can go by unnoticed. Consider being more firm with someone who owes you money. You cannot afford to have outstanding debts.

Tuesday the 7th. Risk taking is not a good idea today. Tread carefully in any business dealings. You can be more impressive in negotiations if you take a cautious approach. Single Scorpio is advised not to waste time with someone who is reluctant to make a commitment. It may be best to issue an ultimatum and stick to it.

Wednesday the 8th. Noisy neighbors could prove troublesome today. If this is an ongoing situation, it is best to nip the situation in the bud. You may not feel much like traveling now. But if business is involved, you are likely to benefit by a face-to-face meeting. You seem to be ready to have a social evening.

Weekly Summary

A health problem could be of concern toward the beginning of this week. If you haven't had a checkup in a while, one is probably in order. Taking care of yourself physically is important now. You have a busy week and need all your powers of concentration. Activities centering around the Fourth of July holiday can keep you going. You will find, however, that relaxing with festivities will give you a needed lift.

You are no doubt enjoying a creative streak this week. Special interests you pursue now can offer possible future benefits. Your self-confidence can inspire those around you as you set an example to others. This week is likely to be a turning point in a romantic affair. Do not feel guilty if the relationship is not working out. Your intuition will lead you to the right decision.

Financial or business matters are not likely to be a problem if you realize that risks may be involved. Careful investigation will get you the results you want. It will probably be necessary to persevere if you want to get a loan repaid. A firm approach is the answer. This is not the time to let someone off the hook.

28th Week/July 9–15

Thursday the 9th. This is a favorable day for developing future career plans. Do not lose sight of current obligations, however. It is important to get your priorities right. Try to avoid getting carried away on a shopping trip. It should really be just for routine items. You may need to drag yourself away from conversations with gossipy neighbors.

Friday the 10th. Make a new start where business and personal plans are concerned. You have an excellent chance of striking up good relations with new contacts. This is likely to be especially helpful for Scorpio working in sales or public relations who's looking for new clients. Keep an eye on household appliances. A large item may need servicing sooner than you think.

Saturday the 11th. Be prepared for a variety of disruptions to your schedule. Unexpected visitors could be knocking at your door. If these are friends from the past, aim to make them welcome. Discussions with a landlord or rental agent are likely to be required. It is important that both sides are living up to their agreements. If you are uncertain, check your obligation.

Sunday the 12th. You are likely to be in an especially lighthearted frame of mind today. You will probably want to get your partner involved in current leisure plans. If you are organizing a party for later in the week, do the planning together. There is no real need for you to take on too many burdens single-handedly at the present time.

Monday the 13th. Bosses are likely to leave you more to your own devices. Try to use your time constructively. Take the opportunity to get a little personal work out of the way. Routine duties should not be neglected, however. Working quickly and efficiently will bring good results and give you the time to do everything you want to do.

Tuesday the 14th. It will probably irritate you if you find out that your mate has been a little too free and easy with spending lately. Discuss the matter calmly, however. It is possible that he or she has spent on something as a surprise for you. Children's activities are likely to be costly. Consider what is affordable and make a choice among your options.

Wednesday the 15th. Keep an eye on the future. This is a favorable time for making long-term plans. Try to avoid paying a great deal of attention to details at this stage. It is probably better to focus primarily on your vision for the future. You are likely to want to cut corners at work. Think carefully before you proceed. It could backfire on you at some later point.

Weekly Summary

This is a week for treading a fine line between keeping one eye on the present and another on the future. It is important to set your priorities. There is a tendency at the moment for you to go to extremes in some respects. Instead, focus on necessities. Leave luxury shopping until another time. Stick to purchasing what you really need at home for the time being.

New beginnings are the order of the day this week.

In the business world you are likely to make some new contacts who will be helpful to you in the future. Socially, also, you should be making new friends and acquaintances. Although visitors who arrive at your door without an invitation may surprise you, be hospitable. It may well be in your interests to deepen a current friendship or aim for a reunion where an old one is concerned.

Relations with your partner are likely to be up and down. The best part of the week for working and planning together is the latter part of the weekend. At this time you are likely to be very much in tune with each other. It is a good time for making mutual plans and choices together.

29th Week/July 16–22

Thursday the 16th. Make every attempt to get trivial matters out of the way early in the day. You could find yourself short of time for all you want to accomplish. It is vital to organize your time and strive for efficiency. If you grasp an opportunity, you could be in contact with an influential person. A profitable business deal may be in the offing.

Friday the 17th. If you are setting off on a vacation, make sure your home is secure and everything is in order. An early start is advisable. Scorpio planning a vacation should get on the ball. You want to get good accommodations. If children or pets are involved, make sure you have made proper arrangements.

Saturday the 18th. Close relationships tend to be stressful at the moment. Your loved one appears to want to call the shots. This may attitude is not likely to be appealing. Scorpio likes to be in control. Just now it may be better to back down. Try to find out the reason why he or she is being so difficult. A new environment is favored for single Scorpio.

Sunday the 19th. Concentrate on getting your finances in order. Settle accounts and attend to the family budget. There might be a deficiency once you have added everything up. It probably concerns purchases that others have made and forgotten to tell you about. If you are trying to buy or sell property, proceed carefully. Do not give way to ultimatums.

Monday the 20th. A person with a lot of business clout is likely to be helpful with property or financial transactions. This should be a productive day for those of you involved in fund-raising and charity work. A new contact is likely to turn out to be a blessing in disguise. Keep to your agreements, especially on the job or in finances.

Tuesday the 21st. If you need favors from other people, this is the time to ask for them. Do not try to handle too many burdens single-handedly. Your relationship with your loved one is likely to be more enjoyable if you share cultural and social activities together. Focus on the future and beginning a new project or venture. This is a beneficial time to start that diet you may have been postponing.

Wednesday the 22nd. You are probably determined to forge ahead with that new project. You could meet with some resistance from others, however. You do not have to back away. But you will accomplish your goal if you make the proper presentation. Snap up educational opportunities that may come your way.

Weekly Summary

This is a week for getting more on top of situations. This is especially important if you are taking off on vacation near the weekend. If you are still in the planning stage, firm up all arrangements. Take stock of your progress on the job front. Details should be taken care of before you tackle major projects.

Do not necessarily expect total harmony where your love life is concerned. Arguments over mutual decisions could plague your relationship. No doubt there is a reason if your partner is moody or difficult. The problem will not be revealed under pressure but through encouragement and understanding. Single Scorpio needs to get out to new places. The same old scene means meeting the same people. Branch out.

Help from influential people is likely to enhance business or career prospects. Watch for every opportunity. Budgeting can present problems. Avoid overspending. Participating in community activities can bring long-term as well as short-term benefits.

30th Week/July 23–29

Thursday the 23rd. Today marks the beginning of a new chapter in your career life. You may have been temporarily out of work and have had no real success in looking for a new job. This should change now. Alter your tactics. Any offers coming your way should be treated with caution, however. It is likely to be best for you to find out more details before making a commitment.

Friday the 24th. It is advisable to put off making a major career decision until you feel more certain about the right choice. Do not give in to pressure from those around you unless there really is no other option. It is well to consider family obligations in planning for the future. This is especially important if you are thinking of accepting an offer that will involve a move.

Saturday the 25th. This is another favorable day for career planning. It is likely that an individual of some considerable influence in the business world will be of help to you. If you are attending an important function, do make an effort to look your best. First impressions are likely to count. Do not waste time hesitating over opportunities that are clearly golden.

Sunday the 26th. Get out and do something different today. Travel is highlighted. You are likely to have a particularly enjoyable time if friends are involved. Look to the future and broaden your horizons. A partner may not be very supportive. Try to find out why. It could be that he or she is insecure and not does not feel fully included in your plans. Aim to share more.

Monday the 27th. This is one of those days when you are at risk of being talked into something you really do not want to do. A friend who criticizes you, even in a lighthearted way, for backing out of a plan may not be respecting your choices. Make it clear if you feel offended. Social activities this evening with congenial companions should help to improve your outlook.

Tuesday the 28th. Make it a point of spending as much time alone as possible today. You are likely to get less done when you are around other people. A problem can probably be solved quite easily if you give sufficient thought to it. Other people's guidance may be helpful. But their advice probably does not provide the answers you are looking for. Seek answers inside yourself.

Wednesday the 29th. You could be feeling under the weather today. Strenuous activities are not advisable. A possible commitment to a trip may have to be canceled or postponed. If a friend is involved, he or she is sure to understand. It may be necessary to take off from work. You cannot be productive when you feel ill.

Weekly Summary

Your career should take a turn for the better this week. It is an especially promising time for Scorpio looking for new work. Opportunities that have not been available before are likely to start cropping up. Efforts you have put in during the past few months appear to be paying off. Be careful not to make moves too early, however. You could be uncertain at first about which choice of several is the right one.

First impressions are likely to count for a lot this week. This is especially true for those of you attending job interviews. Make an effort to be well groomed. You could be invited to an important social function where there is someone you want to make a good impression on. Consider carefully your initial approach. The right introduction is important.

Balance leisure time this week. You probably want to be sociable. But you also need to rest and relax in the interest of your well-being. This appears to be a time when you want to be more alone. If you must socialize, do so quietly and with one or two enjoyable friends.

31st Week/July 30–August 5

Thursday the 30th. The advice of older and wiser individuals is likely to be invaluable. A problem can be resolved more quickly if you listen to experienced people. You may feel you have not been entirely honest with a loved one. If so, correct the situation right away and set your conscience at rest.

Friday the 31st. You are unlikely to see eye-to-eye with colleagues and superiors today. Trust your own judgment. Some direction has probably been helpful recently, but you know better about certain matters. Expect a visit from someone you have not seen in a long time. This could cause you some confusion. Take time to think about an offer or proposition that may result.

Saturday August 1st. You have not had the easiest of times in recent days. Enjoyable entertainment could be just the ticket to relieve the stresses and strains. Your creative impulses should be acted upon. Perhaps begin some new studies or pick up an old hobby. If you have had plans to redecorate a room in your house, reconsider them now.

Sunday the 2nd. Positive financial developments are highlighted. Take time to balance your personal and family accounts. If you are having problems with money, it might be worthwhile getting some expert advice. Make a list of trustworthy people you could contact. Do not rush in where property matters are concerned. It is in your best interests to consider your decision carefully.

Monday the 3rd. Be patient where real estate matters may be pending. It is likely to be difficult to pin others down to commitments. You generally prefer to be in control. But in joint situations, the decision making must be agreed upon mutually. Listen to your own intuition rather than rely on the advice of some friends who claim to know it all. You probably know better.

Tuesday the 4th. You may be seeking an investment or need to borrow funds. If so, your best course is probably to consult an expert. References from people in the know could help you make the right choice. Be sure you have a sound plan to present. Take time to enjoy an evening out with good friends or loved ones.

Wednesday the 5th. This should be an easygoing day when you are left more to your own devices. At work you will probably be able to set your own schedule. If you are self-employed, less interruptions from the outside mean that you are able to get on with in-depth planning. Make a point of catching up on correspondence that has been neglected lately.

Weekly Summary

People with more experience or professional expertise are likely to figure in your plans this week. Advice on investments or business ventures is important if you are to make the right moves. On the job, you can trust your own talents and experience. Decisions you make will head you in the right direction.

Personal money matters can progress positively. It is a good idea to settle personal accounts. If any long-term problems are plaguing you, get outside advice. Those in the know can help you come up with solutions. Major investments need careful thought. Give yourself plenty of leeway to conclude any deals.

The pressures of everyday life can be relieved by enjoying the company of loved ones. You can get a whole new perspective by indulging in entertainments you like. A comedy film or play is sure to pick up everyone's spirits. If possible, get together with younger people. They have much to offer.

32nd Week/August 6–12

Thursday the 6th. An invigorating day appears to lie ahead of you. A social invitation that comes your way is likely to be tempting. This is also a good time for issuing your own invitations. Involvement in sports and physical activities should be enlivening. Make a point of doing something to get more involved in your local community.

Friday the 7th. It may not be easy to keep the peace at home today. Your partner appears to want the upper hand. If you do not want any trouble, give in to his or her whims this time around. It is important now to divide your time evenly between business interests and domestic affairs. Open discussion of any conflicts will help to smooth them over.

Saturday the 8th. It is likely that you will be feeling a little under par today. Quite likely, nothing is really serious. It is probably just a matter of relaxing more and recharging your batteries. Try not to become agitated or frustrated over matters that you have no way to control. Relax and trust that others will do what they can to make things go your way.

Sunday the 9th. This is not a good day for taking risks. Avoid making precarious speculations. You probably have more to gain by being cautious and reserved. A romantic involvement may be rewarding. But it is likely to be taking its toll in time spent in the relationship. Be careful that you do not overextend yourself. More balance in your relationship is likely to be the answer.

Monday the 10th. This should be a creative and enterprising day. It is a good idea to involve yourself more in personal projects. It may even be possible to turn a personal interest into a lucrative business proposition. This is a better day for taking risks than yesterday. A small speculation should do no harm, provided you can back it up without dipping into capital.

Tuesday the 11th. Stick to routine now. It is a good idea to get pressing responsibilities out of the way early in the day. Not too much else should distract you at that time. A business deal is likely to be concluded more easily than you expect, without a hitch. Good relations with colleagues tend to make life on the job a lot more pleasurable.

Wednesday the 12th. There is a possibility of worrying too much about your health today. You may not exactly be feeling in top form. But this does not have to mean that anything is seriously wrong. Take more exercise if you are feeling sluggish. Work relationships should continue to be good. Acknowledgment from a boss could do a lot to boost your ego.

Weekly Summary

Domestic discords could be wearing this week. It would not be wise to ignore the situation and try to go your own way. Still, you are not likely to make much headway by nagging. Compromise wherever you can. You may be partly at fault for being somewhat neglectful. Keep in mind that personal relationships are as important to your well-being as success in other areas.

A social whirl is not advised. You could, however, play host for a quiet get-together with those close to you. More rest is probably the answer to certain stresses and strains. This could be the answer if you are not feeling at your best. Restless Scorpio could benefit by focusing on developing future business plans. Find the time to work on a special project. Involve someone you trust. Together you might realize a profit.

A tempting offer to speculate could come your way. The risks involved are probably not worth the investment. You may need to be more cautious when it comes to spending. Large-ticket items may have to be put off for a time. Professional opportunities are likely to open up, giving your self-confidence a lift.

33rd Week/August 13–19

Thursday the 13th. A close friendship seems to be under some strain. The other's actions and reactions are rather hard to predict. You are apt to allow your naturally suspicious nature to send you off into unreal imaginings. Easing the conflict between you could be accomplished if each allows the other more freedom.

Friday the 14th. A new romantic partner appears to want to rule the roost. Scorpio prefers to be in control. If the situation is getting out of hand, it may be time to put your foot down. On the work front, you may be facing competition for a promotion or a raise. You could get a step ahead by doing some extra homework.

Saturday the 15th. Business endeavors are likely to be more successful if you opt for a joint venture. Pooling resources can provide the necessary funding for getting started. But be sure that others are committed before plunging in. Be cautious about any property offers. They could be too good to be true.

Sunday the 16th. Scorpio who wants to be involved in community affairs can find the right niche today. Political gatherings or meetings on civic issues appeal to you. If you are known for your activist ideas, prepare to be asked to lead others. Try not to get in over your head, however. You do have other commitments.

Monday the 17th. You could be called on to do some long-distance traveling. This may not be a good time. But you would be wise to comply. Others are looking at your potential, and you can make a good impression. Pay attention to the pros and cons of a possible financial deal. Others may have their own axe to grind.

Tuesday the 18th. Concentrate on broadening your horizons, professionally and personally. An interesting educational opportunity may arise now. It could be just right for you. Overseas contacts are likely to be fortunate. Look to your long-term future when you are planning. It might be helpful to get involved in training programs if they are offered.

Wednesday the 19th. If you cannot get away right now for a vacation, you might consider a few days' break. Plan something for the weekend. Try to get out and find a spot that appeals to you. This is a good time to avoid office politics. Others may want to involve you in gossip. Do not believe all you hear.

Weekly Summary

It is likely that a love affair or marriage is still a source of stress. Your partner may want things to go all his or her own way. You probably do not want to stand in the way of your loved one's plans. But you also need to look after your own interests. It could be that you both should be more independent.

Joint endeavors are highlighted in other areas of your life this week. Success is likely to come in the business world when you pool resources. Property deals may not be all you think. So be sure to investigate any offers thoroughly. Public affairs are likely to take up some of your time now. You seem eager this week to be involved with others in group efforts.

A welcome change of pace may come with a long-distance trip. You can benefit in the future by making the best possible impression. Professionally, you stand to gain by thinking big. Others may present some obstacles. But you are self-confident now, and appear to have let your ambitions rule you now.

34th Week/August 20–26

Thursday the 20th. Expect the unexpected. The clearer your schedule is in the first place, the easier it will be to take on board changes of plan. Bosses do not appear to be in a position to reveal all at the moment. Try to be patient. If you do not receive much praise for your efforts, it is probably more of an oversight than a reflection of your work.

Friday the 21st. Do not waste your time trying to please people who simply will not be satisfied. There are better ways of utilizing your energies. Patience appears to be a virtue just now. Before too long, you should actually receive the acknowledgment you deserve. Sit tight. Tonight's New Moon will usher in some changes that will benefit you very soon.

Saturday the 22nd. Make a point of getting together with friends and acquaintances whose company you enjoy. This is a favorable time for giving a dinner party or house party. You should find that people who have not met before, including the spouses of friends, get along well together. Be careful how you spend money today. You will quickly regret going over your budget.

Sunday the 23rd. Romantic undertones in one of your friendships may not be a welcome development. If too much was said last night, in the heat of the moment or after a lot to drink, do not worry. You will be able to smooth the situation over today. It is best not to let things develop in the wrong direction, though. This might happen if you say nothing about the incident.

Monday the 24th. It is another favorable day for getting together with friends and community contacts. Make a point of catching up with people with whom you have been out of touch for a while. Something pleasant is likely to arrive in the mail today. If it is a gift of some kind, perhaps free tickets to a special event, send a thank-you or make a telephone call right away.

Tuesday the 25th. Your day should go smoothly if you are involved more in behind-the-scenes activities. Good progress can be made, especially in the work arena. If you have been temporarily out of work, make a point of getting in touch with past contacts. A friend in your field could have some leads. Your boss is likely to be taking note of what you are doing today. Stay on top of the work.

Wednesday the 26th. Tie up loose ends and get old projects and paperwork out of the way once and for all. You may have moved quite recently and are having your mail redirected. Be sure to write to the people who are still contacting you at the old address. Friendships should be harmonious and pleasant. Partners are likely to be extra supportive and understanding.

Weekly Summary

It seems that no matter how hard you work at it this week you have trouble pleasing others. You may be trying too hard. Keep in mind that those around you cannot always be attentive to your wishes. Patience is required. With some people, however, you could be wasting your time. You need to distinguish between what is real and what you may be imagining.

Friends are likely to be a source of enjoyment now. Socializing can be relaxing and ease some of the tensions. If you are confused about the attentions of someone, it will be best to clear the air. You may have gotten a bit carried away and sent some mixed signals. Avoid confiding in anyone else.

Professional or business associates can be helpful to you this week. Making contacts can give you some new ideas and bring future benefits. Not everything you do should be out in the open. Some situations probably have to be handled with secrecy. Any major changes or moves require organization. Make sure everything is in order before you press ahead.

35th Week/August 27–September 2

Thursday the 27th. Take more initiative in career or business affairs. You should meet with positive responses. Superiors or associates may not condone your actions if you go ahead on your own. Get approval before making any major moves. You might benefit more by presenting ideas rather than carrying them out.

Friday the 28th. A lack of confidence from others should not deter you from your personal plans. Family or friends seem to feel you are going overboard. Trust your own judgment and instincts. You do not always have to play by the rule book. Let others be cautious. You know what is better for you now.

Saturday the 29th. Today you will probably be able to call the shots. Plans have come to fruition, and others are impressed. A mate or lover seems ready to fall in line with your desires. You may have found that a health concern was only a minor problem. Take advantage of your relief by an evening of social fun.

Sunday the 30th. You seem to have budgeted well recently. Do not be surprised if you find some extra money. Reward yourself by getting that something special you want. If it is a household item, you could get lucky and find a bargain. You might want to spruce up your image. Try a new hairdo or some new clothes.

Monday the 31st. Financial developments now could change your attitude toward money. Scorpio is not generally materially motivated. But you do like the status that money brings. Past efforts have put you in a position to receive the reward you had hoped for. Use it to enjoy more of what you want.

Tuesday September 1st. You are likely to be in for a lively and convivial day. Get in touch with old friends and take advantage of any opportunity to make new contacts. Other people are sure to be helpful if you need favors. What you say in the work place is likely to be more important than what you do. Give clear instructions.

Wednesday the 2nd. This should be another enjoyable day. Make the most of the chance to indulge in new leisure activities. Sports or some outdoor pastimes should be particularly stimulating. If you are alone, visit someone who is also alone. Speak your mind at work. If you have good ideas for improvements, make them known.

Weekly Summary

You can make greater strides this week in your business or career life. It is to your advantage to speak up and be more aggressive. Others may not always agree. But you can persuade them if you prove that your ideas and actions are to everyone's benefit. Let your self-confidence show. You should be able to count on the support of influential people.

Toward the end of the week, you should be enjoying a social atmosphere. Activities in the company of others are sure to stimulate you in mind and body. Making advantageous contacts is also likely. Let those around you know that you are open to new ideas. Look for the possible granting of a favor.

Monetary rewards can be yours this week. Financially, you are in a good position. Spending for some of the things you want will not break the bank. Get together with a loved one and share your ideas. There should be no problem in deciding on what will please both of you.

36th Week/September 3–9

Thursday the 3rd. You may not feel like getting out of bed and going to work today. Your attitude is probably due more to a lack of enthusiasm than feeling unwell. Make every effort to show up, however. You could be surprised at how stimulating the day can be. Renew your efforts to make contacts if you are unemployed.

Friday the 4th. For some Scorpio, the upcoming Labor Day weekend may mean travel. Visiting friends or relatives gives you a much-needed break. If you are getting an early start, make sure all arrangements are in order. Staying in familiar surroundings probably appeals to others. Use the time to relax.

Saturday the 5th. Spend time with those you care about today. Young people may need more attention than usual. It will probably be up to you to set an example.

You could find yourself in an awkward situation at a get-together if you encounter someone you would rather not see. You will have to grin and bear it.

Sunday the 6th. If you are home this weekend, it could be a good time to catch up on shopping. There are likely to be some tempting items on sale. Try to be thrifty, however. Right now it would be wise to get only what you need. It may be necessary to meet with a relative to discuss some family business.

Monday the 7th. Take some time today to get in touch with those you have not contacted in a while. Phone calls or visits would be welcome. It could be a nostalgic time reminiscing about old times together. Single Scorpio could have good luck today. Someone you have had an eye on is likely to make an unexpected appearance or phone call.

Tuesday the 8th. Concentrate on getting routine matters sorted out today. A problem is unlikely to be as hard to solve as you imagine. If papers and records are piling up, set about getting them in order. It is likely that colleagues will be willing to lend a hand if you need one. This is a favorable time to set priorities and focus on organizing personal plans. Future benefits may depend on how much you accomplish.

Wednesday the 9th. You should be able to move along quickly with business today. Others are eager to proceed and are impressed with your plans. It could be a long day, however. So be prepared to answer any and all questions. If you have to travel, take the shortest route. You do not need to be caught in traffic.

Weekly Summary

You should get a much-needed break this week because of the holiday. It seems as if you have not been too highly motivated recently. Your outlook probably needs perking up. Whether you travel or stay at home, a respite from the demands of job or business is a chance to renew your spirits. Surround yourself with those you care about. The activities of young people can be especially enjoyable.

Work can ease up toward the end of the week when colleagues cooperate. Making a project a group effort will get details out of the way quickly. Try to make sure that superiors are aware of your abilities. Contacts you make this week are likely to put you in a better position professionally. But you probably need to make more of an effort to get in touch with people.

Too much spending at this time is not advisable. Pay more attention to what you are buying. Eye-catching items may not be the bargains you think they are. Romance could be on the menu for single Scorpio. And it can come just when you are ready for a new relationship. Contacts from the past can bring pleasant memories.

37th Week/September 10–16

Thursday the 10th. It will probably be difficult to keep out of an argument with a partner. He or she may be critical in what you feel are minor matters. Instead of flying off the handle, discuss the problem rationally. You will not be doing yourself a favor by overlooking the situation. Single Scorpio should not come on too strongly. The approach may not be appreciated.

Friday the 11th. This appears to be the time to sort out differences on the job front. Apparently your ideas do not coincide with those of your co-workers. Try not to involve superiors. Straighten out any conflicts among yourselves. Avoid getting into financial dealings with friends. It could backfire.

Saturday the 12th. Joint ventures need extra care. The advice of others may be helpful. If you have too many points of view, however, it could be confusing. Listen to the person with the most business sense. You are likely to be in competition with others if you are looking for property. Be prepared to do battle.

Sunday the 13th. Your mood indicates that a change of scenery is likely to be beneficial. Try to arrange an outing. You may think you want to be alone. But good company could make a jaunt more enjoyable. If you cannot get away, reconsider a special interest you may have dropped. Volunteer work is a gift you can give.

Monday the 14th. Self-promotion is the name of the game today. Others need to know you are around. If you are going to meet with others, blow your own horn. The key to success in a possible new business venture is imaginative advertising. And strong promotion of a product can increase your current business prospects.

Tuesday the 15th. Good friends tend to bring out the best in you at the moment. You seem to be in great demand. Take advantage of the atmosphere to plan a dinner or party. Teamwork is the key to accomplishment now. A project dear to your heart can progress well when everyone works together. An unusual invitation can be accepted if you discard preconceived ideas.

Wednesday the 16th. All the efforts you have been putting in at work recently should start paying off now.

Some kind of reward or acknowledgment is likely from your boss or employer. If you employ other people, why not give those who deserve it a pat on the back? An incentive to boost production is likely to be a good investment.

Weekly Summary

A personal relationship could prove to be touchy this week. A loved one seems to be acting somewhat out of character. You may feel that your independence is at stake. Before you take any actions you could regret, calm down. Your vivid imagination may have blown the situation out of proportion. There is little that an open and honest talk cannot clear up. Friends are especially enjoyable this week. Time you spend with them lifts your spirits.

You need to be on the ball this week where work is concerned. Much can be accomplished if everyone pulls together. It may take all your diplomatic skills to create the right environment. When you do, you can take pride in the final outcome. Rewards are sure to come. If you are still waiting for the big break, take every opportunity to promote yourself.

Success in business depends a great deal on you. This is the week to let your imagination take hold. Scorpio can be very adventurous when the time demands it. There is little risk involved in trying new ideas in advertising or giving incentives to others. Some caution is required, however, in any financial dealings. You may want to consider some outside advice.

38th Week/September 17–23

Thursday the 17th. This looks like a favorable day for expanding career interests. If you want to get into another branch of your profession, perhaps a training course would help. Evening classes could also be useful. Aim at adding another string to your bow. There should be more time for thinking and planning today. You will have few interruptions.

Friday the 18th. Make a point of getting together with friends this evening for some light entertainment. If you have not been to the theater or a musical event in a while, make reservations. It is likely to take you out of yourself. Do remember anniversaries of people you care about. A card arriving at just the right time is likely to give a great deal of pleasure.

Saturday the 19th. An impromptu get together with good friends is likely to be very enjoyable this weekend. If you are trying to lose weight at the moment, it can be encouraging to do so with a group. Consider joining a swimming club. This is a favorable time for picking up a hobby you have enjoyed in the past but neglected. You might involve a loved one in a favorite project.

Sunday the 20th. Greater mental stimulation is likely to be what is needed today. Perhaps go along to a talk or seminar on a subject that interests you. For single Scorpio, pursuing your personal interests could very well lead to a romantic meeting. Where group entertainments are concerned, try not to favor someone who is being a bit selfish.

Monday the 21st. If you have a busy day lined up, try to fit in a break. A walk at lunchtime could do you a world of good. You may not be paying enough attention to your health. Cutting back on a rich diet is also a good idea. You could become frustrated if you have to change your schedule. Take it in stride. You do not need any additional stress.

Tuesday the 22nd. Concentrate on professional objectives today. You appear to have routine matters in hand and can focus on long-term plans. Let others know you do not want interruptions and distractions. An event behind the scenes could have an impact on your personal life. A friend may clue you in to what is happening.

Wednesday the 23rd. Your wish for peace and quiet is not likely to be granted today. People who may not be aware of your desire to be alone could be making demands on your time. You are not in the mood to listen to the complaints of others, or even to engage in frivolous conversation. Put your foot down once and for all.

Weekly Summary

You can make considerable headway with career plans this week. If you want to move up, training courses could be the answer. Do not hesitate to ask for managerial training. Consider also education courses in your field that may be available. When Scorpio is determined to move ahead, there is little that will deter you.

Group activities are enjoyable this week. Get-togethers with friends or family offer an opportunity to get away from routine. It appears that you are interested in light entertainment that is affordable. You are not going to spend a fortune for a movie or the theater. There will be times, however, when you want to be alone. This could prove difficult when others interrupt or distract you. You have to let them know you need rest and quiet.

During the weekend you want mental stimulation. This may lead you to pursue a more serious interest or course of study. For single Scorpio, getting involved in a special interest could mean meeting someone new. Paying more attention to your health may lead to following a better diet and getting more exercise. Even short breaks for a brisk walk can pay off in more energy and endurance.

39th Week/September 24–30

Thursday the 24th. Make a fresh start with personal plans today. You could find that you are left more to your own devices than was possible yesterday. Careful self-examination is likely to be valuable in making a decision that has been troubling you. Do not take on projects that look too hard to handle. If you are unsure, possibly it is because you are trying to prove something.

Friday the 25th. If you are going for a job interview today, do not be afraid to put your best foot forward. Express just how good you are at what you do. This is a favorable day for letting others know your skills. You ought to be able to make some important social and business connections today. Bear in mind that first impressions are often the ones that count the most.

Saturday the 26th. There is likely to be a lot going on around you now. Do not expect to have a quiet and uneventful day. Someone paying you a compliment is likely to boost your ego. If you are going to a special event this evening, make an effort to dress the part. Once again, good impressions count for a lot at the moment. Stun everybody!

Sunday the 27th. This is one of those days when you can get dragged into lending money to someone. Your instinct is to say no. But the saying about "a friend in need" will probably be going through your mind. You probably should consider just how often this friend is actually in need. If you feel this is one too many times, it is undoubtedly best to find an excuse not to lend.

Monday the 28th. Do talk about problems with your loved one today. What you discuss is likely to leave you feeling much more reassured about a situation that has been bothering you. This looks like a very good time for making mutual plans together. If you are single, be prepared to strike up an interesting conversation with somebody new.

Tuesday the 29th. Relationships can be deepened and consolidated today. It is a favorable time for networking and meeting new people. If your body is feeling sluggish, consider getting in some sports practice. If you do not enjoy any sports on a regular basis, perhaps this is a good time to begin. Time spent in relaxing is also likely to be pleasant and refreshing.

Wednesday the 30th. This is a propitious day for joint financial undertakings. There could be problems with the legal elements of a contract, however. Try not to worry too much about a situation you cannot control. If you are struggling to get some work finished, get those around you in on the act. You will probably reduce your work load far more than you expect.

Weekly Summary

The overall focus this week is very much on your inner life, dreams, and schemes. This should be a good time for putting personal plans into action. It is likely to be to your advantage to take your time over making a major decision. Nobody should be rushing you, so take it easy.

Your work prospects seem to be improving. For

Scorpio who has been temporarily out of work, this is a key week for getting your face known in new companies. Be sure the person you are seeing is aware of your special skills. It might be wise to redo a resume. If you are self-employed, focus on greater publicity to attract new clients. Having too much work to do can be stressful. Ask others to lend a hand.

Where personal relationships are concerned, you should see some positive developments. Your partner is likely to be a great support at the moment. Look to the future and do some planning together. For single Scorpio, the chances of meeting a new partner are better than usual after the weekend. Someone introduced to you via a friend could turn out to be very much on the same wavelength with you. Your body probably needs new energy. Get in better shape with exercise.

40th Week/October 1–7

Thursday October 1st. Behind-the-scenes involvements are favored on the work front. Make every attempt to keep out of tricky situations that may arise. Maintain a low profile. Money matters can be of some concern now. If you have debts, consider a consolidation loan. Expect good news in a possible property deal.

Friday the 2nd. Your more innovative ideas are likely to meet with a good response today. Broadcast them. Set new schemes in action. Avoid being stuck in a rut of your own making. If you have noticed that you have been putting on weight, resolve to put a stop to it now. Perhaps buy a book or video on a new type of diet and exercise regime. If this does not appeal to you, exercise willpower.

Saturday the 3rd. This should be a relaxing weekend. Take time out to put your feet up and let the world pass you by. The worries that have been on your mind during the week can be temporarily cast aside. If you have children, take them out somewhere that is fun. It could recharge your energy. It will probably help if it is a place you would like to visit too.

Sunday the 4th. This is a favorable day for making more contact with others. If a birthday, anniversary, or other occasion is coming up, send a card or make a call. Relatives are sure to appreciate hearing from you, especially if you have been out of touch for a while. Your writing skills could come in handy now.

Monday the 5th. Push aside all obstacles and determine to clear away neglected tasks. Professionally, it is a good idea to put a new routine in place. If problems seem to be brewing with colleagues, handle the situation right away. If you dawdle, it could escalate. A windfall could be yours with little risk.

Tuesday the 6th. This is one of those days when things can go wrong because of crossed wires, especially at work. Double-check information passed your way. Pay particular attention to telephone messages. Try not to make assumptions. You could end up having an embarrassing few moments. If you are given a document to approve, read through it carefully before signing.

Wednesday the 7th. You are likely to make a breakthrough in a relationship that has been difficult in the recent past. Either your partner or you will realize that you have both reached the point of no return. There are probably going to be a few surprises at home. A loved one may have kept some private plans hidden and now they will be revealed. You should be in for a nice surprise.

Weekly Summary

You should benefit by maintaining a fairly low profile at work before you go for the kill and bombard everyone with your latest new plans. Concentrate on clearing a backlog out of the way before moving on to something more exciting. Once you get going on your new schemes, there is no reason to hold back. Self-promotion appears to be your key to success. If you are in sales it is likely to be conscientious marketing that brings a new contract your way.

The weekend is a time for rest and relaxation. Make your pleasures light and fun filled. Children may want to be taken out. If so, find a place where you do not necessarily have to keep a constant eye on them. If you wish to pursue your own leisure activities, try to get outdoors. Some good exercise will tone up your body.

Make more effort to contact people you have neglected. Your social life should pep up, especially after the weekend. Relatives who live at a distance can be forgotten in the grand scheme of things. Make every effort not to overlook an important date such as a birthday or wedding anniversary.

41st Week/October 8–14

Thursday the 8th. Your past experience is likely to be helpful when you apply it to a current relationship or business situation. Be wise and realistic. There is little point in pretending that the scenario is working out well if it is not. If you want to give a love relationship a boost, do more romantic things. Talk about your hopes and wishes.

Friday the 9th. A joint financial situation is likely to improve if you do your best to make the facts and details clearer. Look forward to the possibility of promising news in relation to a property deal. A contract could even be drawn up. Keep ongoing negotiations quiet. It is probably best to play your cards close to your chest than to reveal too much too soon.

Saturday the 10th. An oversight on the part of a financial planner or business adviser is likely to come to light today. The situation ought to turn around in your favor, even though initially it may look quite precarious. Do all you can to let others know you care about them. Spend some time today talking about the future with your loved one.

Sunday the 11th. You may not feel up to making a long trip that has been planned. See if you can wiggle your way out of going. Close friends are likely to be understanding. Take something that you read with a grain of salt. This is a time when both what is written and what is spoken can be oddly misleading. Trust your own intuition and judgment much more.

Monday the 12th. Do not panic if something you have hoped would happen does not. It may become quite plain to you that, in fact, it never will. There is time for another plan to be hatched. Let your imagination run riot. You have an especially creative sense just now. It is a good idea to begin a new hobby or project. There is very little reason to be really down for long.

Tuesday the 13th. It is likely to be more important than usual to put on a professional front at work today. This is also true for Scorpio who may be going for interviews or attending conferences. Do not let your guard down. You and a superior probably will not agree on a central matter. It is as well to bite your tongue, however. Saying too much could work against you.

Wednesday the 14th. You should be able to make some marked progress with business and professional affairs today. If you are self-employed, this is likely to be a surprisingly productive day. Make the most of opportunities to settle problems behind closed doors. Where possible legal issues are concerned, an out-of-court settlement will most probably be in your favor.

Weekly Summary

Look to the past to guide your future this week. Old contacts could be a help to you. Most of all, the ability to fall back on past experience should save you from making a mistake on an important work project. Wisdom and realism are your keys to success in the business world. Try to avoid taking on more than you can comfortably handle. Bear in mind that although a challenge is stimulating, stress can be draining.

For those of you thinking about buying or selling property, developments are likely to be heartening. Joint purchases in particular are favored. If you are buying alone, your best bet is to keep your own counsel. The advice of others could be misleading. Your interests will probably be served in any legal matters if a settlement is proposed.

Loved ones are likely to play an important part in your life this week. Someone very close to you seems to need reassurance. You may have been neglectful in including him or her in your future plans. You can be imaginative and creative this week. Use these talents to do something you have been thinking about.

42nd Week/October 15–21

Thursday the 15th. This is not one of the best times to get involved in financial dealings with friends. You probably should consider the effect that a business or financial contract could have on your relationship in the future. Try to avoid making snap decisions. You could regret doing so at some later point in time. Be sure to think things through carefully.

Friday the 16th. This looks like a good day for focusing on your personal plans. You should have more time on your hands to do as you please. On the job front, you are likely to find that teamwork is your key to success. Try to avoid taking on too much alone. If you want to enhance your social life, consider joining a club where you can meet up with like-minded people.

Saturday the 17th. A special trip is likely this weekend. It is a wonderful time for getting away from your usual surroundings. If you have not seen some of your relatives for a while, consider making a visit. There is little question that your company will be appreciated. Avoid being too inward looking. You can tend to worry too much about situations that will not matter in the future.

Sunday the 18th. Peace and quiet are likely to reign today. You need to rest and relax. Others appear to have their own interests to pursue. If you like to write, it may be the time to plan out that article or story you have been mulling over. A walk in the crisp air or by the water could be just the right tonic.

Monday the 19th. It looks as though you are in for another quiet day. Take advantage of the opportunity to catch up on neglected tasks. Involvement in behind-the-scenes work ought to be profitable. Single Scorpio may feel nervous about getting to know someone who seems somewhat unapproachable. Give this person a chance. He or she might just be a bit shy.

Tuesday the 20th. It looks as though you are beginning a new chapter where your well-being is concerned. Now is the time to begin practicing a more healthy regimen. Make time for exercise. Pay more attention to your diet and eating habits. Behavior is not always easy to change, but Scorpio is a determined person.

Wednesday the 21st. Increased energy today is bound to help you achieve more than you set out to do. Your confidence is also likely to be on the rise. Perhaps pursue some of your more ambitious goals. If you want others to leave you alone, be firm about letting them know. Too many distractions could put you out of sorts.

Weekly Summary

Be careful of mixing business and friendship this week. If you are contemplating a financial venture, look for support elsewhere. Your friends probably do not want to offend you. But you could find them avoiding your company if you try to involve them in something they do not want to do. You are likely to be successful by making contacts outside your social circle.

Taking on too much responsibility by yourself is not advisable. You could get in over your head. On the job, try to delegate duties. Associates appear to be supportive of new projects. Make the work a group effort. Your energy level will likely be high toward the end of the week. Use it to advance your objectives.

The weekend offers a chance to relax and follow your own pursuits. A trip could get you away from routine. Visiting those you have not seen for a while will be a welcome change. A new love interest could enter your life if you give someone the chance. A change in some habits could enhance your well-being and boost self-confidence as well as your image.

43rd Week/October 22–28

Thursday the 22nd. Look for tangible results today. You probably cannot believe all that you are told. Visible evidence is likely to be much more convincing. Somebody may let you down at the last minute. Although you may be angry, listen to the other person's reason. It is more likely to be just an oversight on his or her part rather than a lack of consideration.

Friday the 23rd. If you are involved in property negotiations, expect some positive results. Those of you interested in a new business opportunity would probably be wise to carry out some initial research. Your partner may not agree with your plans at the moment. It is probably best to discuss the matter in more depth. Going ahead on your own could cause conflict.

Saturday the 24th. Keep an eye on spending today. Social activities could put a strain on your budget. Avoid a round of parties. You will be apt to let work pile up and regret it later. Someone may be taking you for granted and needs to be set straight. If a separation is in order, you will have to decide.

Sunday the 25th. If you wish to gain support with your plans, approach the right person or people early in the day. A journey undertaken with your loved one is likely to be exciting. This is a good day for making all sorts of plans for the future together. For single Scorpio, a long-distance journey could lead to a meeting with someone special.

Monday the 26th. You may meet your work goals today if you suggest a team effort. Others will probably need guidance but appear cooperative. A possible new financial venture is likely to require the contributions of several others. Organize your ideas and plans and present them. This could be the right day to make new contacts.

Tuesday the 27th. Although yesterday was favorable for expanding your contacts, today looks to be somewhat different. In meetings or discussions, you may wonder if you are involving the right people. You might rethink your plans. You could decide it is better to stick to working with people who are familiar.

Wednesday the 28th. It looks as though there will be a few surprises in store for you today. You will probably cope best with any change of plan if your schedule is not too full in the first place. At home you can be a trial to be around because you feel restless and edgy. Try not to take out your temporary bad temper on your nearest and dearest.

Weekly Summary

For the most part, you will have few major problems to deal with this week. Business or property opportunities can produce tangible results. You will probably have to make an important decision about involving others in your plans. A group effort on the job front can get the work done on schedule. You will probably be required to give guidance to others.

Money needs to be carefully handled this week. The temptation to indulge in a social whirl should be avoided. Your personal budget appears to be too tight now. Plans for a financial venture should be organized. The contributions of others are probably necessary. They will want to know you are on the right track.

Not all personal relationships are likely to meet your expectations. Do not be too hasty in forming judgments if you are upset about someone's behavior.

However, there may be a situation that you feel cannot continue. If so, follow your intuition. Do not let your irritation spill over to those around you. A loved one can make your day when you travel together on the weekend.

44th Week/October 29–November 4

Thursday the 29th. Do not be surprised if your plans get turned upside down today. It is a time when both new information and sudden news can mean that you need to make some changes. This should, however, help you to get your priorities in order. If you feel insecure at the moment, it is probably just because of a fear of the unknown. This situation could alter very fast.

Friday the 30th. Spend more time today with children. Try to plan some Halloween festivities. You can find that youngsters will be a source of inspiration in thinking of activities. Creative endeavors are highlighted now. Scorpio writers and artists should be able to make excellent progress. Presentations you make are likely to be impressive.

Saturday the 31st. This appears to be a good day to speculate. A new opportunity may seem risky, but think it over. You could have much to gain. Discussions or negotiations may proceed slowly at first. Be patient. It is possible that others involved have not yet sorted out the details and firmed up their plans.

Sunday November 1st. Be prepared for a busy day. Friends or family have plans they want to involve you in. If you have other ideas, go along with those around you. It will please them, and you will be surprised at how much you enjoy yourself. An invitation to a special occasion could come your way.

Monday the 2nd. Make this a day for getting back to routine chores. Direct your efforts to clearing up neglected paperwork or organizing files and records. Detailed and complicated work may need more attention than usual. Household tasks could have piled up. List the most important to accomplish and get at them.

Tuesday the 3rd. The past is likely to catch up with you today. Do not panic if a situation seems to fall apart before your very eyes. It is probably just a matter of taking the time and effort to put things right. Opposition from a loved one is likely. You could quarrel over decoration plans or purchases for the home. Be prepared to compromise.

Wednesday the 4th. Try to create a harmonious environment with your loved one today. He or she appears to be going through a difficult time. Make an effort to be a good friend as well as a lover. Your sympathy and understanding is important in lifting your partner's spirits. Single Scorpio has a surprise in store.

Weekly Summary

Be prepared to deal with some changes during this week. These may not necessarily be to your disadvantage. Try to think of them as a possible blessing in disguise. If you put your mind to it, you can turn them around and probably benefit. Investments or financial matters provide an opportunity to realize a possible gain. These too need careful thought. Consider your future and whether the possible risks are worth taking a chance.

Scorpio can make strides this week in creative endeavors. Those in the literary or artistic fields can be impressive. Ideas seems to flow freely. Others are bound to recognize talent when they see it. You can even find your talents coming to the fore when you get involved in Halloween festivities.

Personal relationships are important to Scorpio this week. A domestic conflict need not be a disaster. All it takes is more understanding and support on your part. You are likely to want to fall in with the plans of those around you. Going along with others provides a pleasant escape. Make time this week to clear up some neglected tasks. Correspondence and other paperwork as well as household chores need clearing up.

45th Week/November 5–11

Thursday the 5th. Joint financial discussions can be tricky today. It would be wise to bring problems out into the open and discuss them fully. This is not the time to rush into investments and long-term commitments. Take your time in making decisions. Explore alternative possibilities where business ventures are concerned. You could come up with some excellent fresh ideas.

Friday the 6th. Check into existing investments to ensure that your interests are being properly taken care of. New information from a different adviser could open your eyes to a subtle trick that has been played on you. However, it is probably not too late to do something about it. Do not make compromises that you are not comfortable with.

Saturday the 7th. It is a good idea to arrange a break from familiar surroundings today. Short trips or visits can refresh your spirits. Important personal affairs may need some further consideration before you come to any conclusions. An educational opportunity that crops up now could help expand your horizons.

Sunday the 8th. Look to the future. This is another favorable day for exploring new horizons. Get together with friends who are likely to encourage and inspire you. Listening to their ideas could start you thinking on a totally different track. For single Scorpio, it is possible that a friendship will turn into a romance, if you want it to happen.

Monday the 9th. Allow for a possible delay in long-distance travel today. The reasons are probably beyond your control. It would still be a good idea, however, to give your car a routine checkup. And make sure other travel arrangements are secure. Scorpio in technical work should ask for what you want. You will be pleased by a thoughtful remembrance of your birthday from someone who once meant a great deal to you.

Tuesday the 10th. Keep personal and career matters separate if you possibly can. Someone higher up is likely to demand an especially professional approach today. Do not expect acceptance if you turn up late or let work lag behind. Try for a change of scene in the middle of the day. A friend could supply a broad shoulder to cry on.

Wednesday the 11th. Sound progress can be made in professional matters today. Events on the job front ought to be smoother going than yesterday. Having cleared up some personal issues, you should feel less hampered and more able to move ahead. This is a good time for attending to neglected tasks. You should be able to finally clear up a long-term problem.

Weekly Summary

Financial interests need careful handling this week if others are involved. Avoid the temptation to keep some information and plans too much of a secret. Any difficulties between you and people involved should be discussed openly. Some investments may present problems that could prevent your reaping proper benefits. Professional affairs present a rosier picture when you keep personal matters from interfering.

A change of scene on the weekend is a good idea. You need a break from the pressures of work and business. Scorpio who is trying to sort out problems will find a break particularly beneficial. Those of you eager to face new challenges can find plenty of opportunities. Travel this week should not present any problems if you have organized and planned well.

Friends provide a cheerful and welcome chance to socialize this week without breaking the bank. Get-togethers will be fun as well as enlightenting. You could find their encouragement sets you to thinking in new ways. A certain friendship may also offer the chance for romance.

46th Week/November 12–18

Thursday the 12th. Try to keep business solely as business today. If you try to mix it with pleasure as well, you could end up with an expansive entertainment bill. Although your generosity may be admirable, it may not be taken in the right spirit. You could find yourself saddled with individuals constantly expecting the same treatment. Start off on the right foot and stay there.

Friday the 13th. This is not likely to be a bad-luck day. Friendships are highlighted. This is an excellent time for making several new contacts and for touching base with old friends. First impressions are likely to count. Be more conscious of grooming and wearing the right outfit for the right occasion. Do discuss your plans and intentions openly with friends and fellow business associates. Allies need to be stroked occasionally.

Saturday the 14th. Keep to your usual routine at home, including settling up any outstanding accounts. You may have to stock up on essentials in the kitchen and the basic, housecleaning items that may have run low. There should be time to take it easy today and fit in some needed relaxation. It is probably a good idea to ensure that your batteries are recharged for the week ahead.

Sunday the 15th. Take a backseat in proceedings today. This is time for slowing down and viewing life from a different perspective. Try to avoid rushing around, attempting to do ten things at once. Special health products are likely to be worth looking into. Concentrate on renewing your energy and generally looking after your well-being.

Monday the 16th. Scandal and gossip seem to surround you at the moment at work. Pay little attention to what you hear. Much of it is probably misguided. Push forward with neglected tasks, especially correspondence and general paperwork. This is a good time for catching up on bills. The more you get out of the way, the more time you should have for new projects.

Tuesday the 17th. Expect some surprises. Interruptions and changes in your regular routine are indicated. Avoid frustration by drawing up a list of your priorities, and get them out of the way first. Grasp a golden opportunity that springs out of nowhere. You may feel neglected early in the day. Things will pick up when you get a call.

Wednesday the 18th. Proceed with confidence today with new ideas. This is a favorable time for personal plans. Spruce up your image. Try experimenting with a new hairdo or a jazzier outfit. Weight may be creeping up, with bulges in all the wrong places. Plan a more careful diet, and get more exercise. Your efforts are sure to be rewarded.

Weekly Summary

Business and pleasure are not a good combination this week. You could be the one who gets stuck footing an expensive bill. If you take advantage of every opportunity, however, new contacts can be important to your future. Keep in mind that to some people appearance is almost more important than experience. It might be a good idea to talk things over with friends or associates.

Use some of the weekend on activities you enjoy doing. You do not always have to be the leader or the one who makes all the arrangements. You will be refreshed physically and mentally if you relax. Time spent is shopping will not tire you out. And you probably need to stock up on some items. You can give a boost to your self-esteem this week by enhancing your personal image. Diet and exercise are important parts of a healthier regimen.

You could be especially sensitive this week to rumors and gossip. Be wary of accepting all you hear or see. You do not want to base decisions on faulty information. Frustration can set in if your routine is interrupted. Be realistic. You may not avoid all distractions. But you can attempt to do the most important things.

47th Week/November 19–25

Thursday the 19th. This is an important day for financial accounting. If you are an employer, be sure that details of your expenses are up to date. Be prepared to present your documents and records for scrutiny. Take time to shop for household items. Look in more than one place. You can probably find things that are both practical and beautiful.

Friday the 20th. Your partner seems determined to spend money on your behalf. Fortunately, he or she will probably consult you first. Put your foot down, however, if you do not feel the purchases are needed or justified. Be on your guard against various forms of emotional blackmail. Someone close to you can be quite manipulative.

Saturday the 21st. You are likely to be busy today. Some well-paid work could come your way, enticing you to give up a weekend of rest and leisure. If it helps to significantly fill your wallet then it will probably be worth the effort. Avoid financial complications in relationships with friends and acquaintances. Their motives may be unclear. Things could get tricky in the future.

Sunday the 22nd. It is likely that you will hear from someone you have not had contact with for a long time. Make this is a day for pleasant reminiscing about the past. Do not get stuck in a rut though. Involve yourself in a community activity. Helping out at a charity function will undoubtedly prove personally rewarding. Perhaps involve family members or friends.

Monday the 23rd. Your work day is likely to be filled with irritating little problems. Resign yourself to the inevitable and cope with them. You may have to confront a colleague who forgot to carry out an assigned task. Double-check to be sure before you speak out. Single Scorpio could be surprised by a communication from a past admirer.

Tuesday the 24th. The long Thanksgiving Day weekend is approaching, and you may not be as prepared as you would like. Use some time today to go over arrangements. If you have procrastinated, you may have to ask for help. It is probably not a good idea to let the job slip. A boss or colleagues are not likely to be too forgiving.

Wednesday the 25th. Family members or friends can be supportive today. They know you have much to do and a lot on your mind. They will understand if you are firm about not being distracted. Make sure business or work is cleared away. It could only be worse if you have to face unfinished business after the holiday.

Weekly Summary

An accounting of finances is likely to be due this week. Get organized as quickly as possible. Go over all documents and records carefully. Situations on the job front can put you in a bad mood. Colleagues may not have lived up to your expectations. Avoid a confrontation if you can. You do not need to get involved in a conflict at this time. For some Scorpio, the weekend could present an opportunity to make some extra money.

The Thanksgiving spirit could prompt you to make contacts with old and new friends. Someone in particular may brighten up your day. You need not limit your socializing. A community activity may appeal to you. Charity functions can be especially rewarding at this time of the year.

Personal or joint finances could present some problems. Money seems to be a bit tight. A spouse or partner may not be aware of too much spending. It is probably time to sit down for a talk. Those around you will make your life easier if you are rushed this week. Do not be reluctant to ask for help. Keep interruptions at a minimum so you can get your work done.

48th Week/November 26–December 2

Thursday the 26th. Happy Thanksgiving! Scorpio's preparations seem to have paid off. It appears that everything has worked out as you planned, even if you had to rush a bit. Express your appreciation if others were of great help to you. You could have a special treat if visitors from afar are included in your festivities.

Friday the 27th. For many this looks to be a day to take it easy. The usual crowd may be eager to get going on Christmas shopping. If you do not feel like facing the crowds, start your list. You will be one step ahead of the game. If you have to work, you can probably get a lot done. The usual crowd may not be around to offer interruptions.

Saturday the 28th. Look for a rewarding day around the home. You seem to have time to work on a neglected do-it-yourself project. Others may want to be involved. But if you want to work alone, avoid any hurt feelings by perhaps suggesting they can help by looking for materials you need. That should do the trick.

Sunday the 29th. This is likely to be a day of surprises. Fortunately they will be pleasant. A financial difficulty will probably pass faster than you expect. Someone may have information about additional work, which could make quite a difference to your overall income. If you have been temporarily out of work, this is a good day for making plans to renew your job-search efforts.

Monday the 30th. Do not expect an easy ride today. Progress at work is likely to be hard going, especially if you have been cutting corners lately. It could take a while to catch up on neglected tasks. It is probably worth putting in an enormous effort to get abreast of the situation. Do something productive to counter the situation if you are concerned about job security.

Tuesday December 1st. Your home life is likely to be rather up and down today. A loved one could be cantankerous. This may very well be because he or she feels pressured and under stress. Try to be supportive. You should find a useful money-earning opportunity coming your way. This ought to help tide you over any financial difficulties you may be currently experiencing.

Wednesday the 2nd. Joint financial matters are highlighted. If you are involved in buying or selling property, it is likely that you will be able to bring negotiations to a positive conclusion. There should be light at the end of the tunnel with regard to an ongoing ordeal. Be watchful of overspending on items that are not really necessities.

Weekly Summary

This week was a time to enjoy a holiday with family or friends. Hosting the activities or visiting others was an opportunity to be in the company of those close to you and possibly renew old friendships. It is likely that the weekend was especially fulfilling when you had time to take on some household projects.

There could be some surprises. But they are not likely to prove insurmountable. A financial problem can be resolved when an opportunity to earn more money may be offered out of the blue. Property or business negotiations can be concluded to your satisfaction. Scorpio looking for a new job may be inspired to renew his or her efforts.

Progress on the job front may not be that easy now. If you have been neglecting tasks or trying to take shortcuts, you could get caught up on it. Let others know your lapse was temporary. A spouse or partner may not see eye-to-eye with you. Getting agreement could prove difficult if you are not understanding. Keep in mind that he or she is also under some pressure. Be reassuring and supportive.

49th Week/December 3–9

Thursday the 3rd. Your routine could be thrown for a loop today. You can make events work for you if you remain flexible. Be creative in scheduling. You may have to involve others in work you cannot get to right away. It is not too early to check your budget for Christmas spending. There could be ways you can save.

Friday the 4th. If you are struggling to get through a long and detailed job at work, do not hesitate to ask for help. Scorpio who is thinking of making a major investment would be wise to begin planning now. Start by making sure your information is sound. A possible joint venture means laying down some ground rules.

Saturday the 5th. A trip may be in the offing today. Family or friends would probably like to join you. If children are on the scene, make it a special day out. Brushing up on a physical activity could overcome any sluggishness you may be feeling. For single Scorpio, an outing could bring an interesting meeting.

Sunday the 6th. You may be thirsting after knowledge today. Consider some study in a field that interests you. A cultural event could be stimulating to your mind and senses. Try to combine an activity with a change of scene. Make the most of an intriguing invitation. It could lead to a surprising conclusion.

Monday the 7th. It would not be wise to rely on influential people to back you today. They may be too involved in other matters to keep their commitment. You will probably have to wait for a better time. Groundwork you lay today in a business proposal can pay off in the long run. Be sure to keep others informed of your plans.

Tuesday the 8th. There are likely to be more opportunities to improve your overall career prospects today. For some Scorpio this could mean considering a move into an entirely different career field. This does not necessarily mean you will have to accept a drop in pay. Influential people appear to be behind you. Their recommendation is in your favor.

Wednesday the 9th. Catch up on personal affairs now. You may have been neglecting those around you. Someone very close could be upset at your absence. If your work has been a top priority recently, make up for it by suggesting more time together. Check your Christmas list. Someone important could be missing from it.

Weekly Summary

Situations on the job front may cause some stress this week. You can, however, overcome obstacles if you remain flexible. Keeping to schedules could be a problem. Avoid frustration by being practical and setting priorities. Others can be of help if you ask. A career change may be in the offing. Consider carefully how any moves will affect your future.

Business or financial affairs are likely to require sound initial planning. It is important to make sure that others who may be involved know the rules of the game. But do not place too much reliance on the support of others. You may have to wait for a firmer commitment. In the long run, however, your efforts can pay off.

The weekend offers the chance to get away from routine. A trip with those near to you can be a special day. Some Scorpio may find physical activity a welcome change. Others are probably more interested in stimulating the mind. Personal relationships could need some fence mending. You may have been too preoccupied lately to notice that others want more of your company.

50th Week/December 10–16

Thursday the 10th. You are likely to be irritated by a friend who does not appear to be giving you due respect and consideration today. This is really no time to allow matters to escalate. Speak your mind, and it should help to clear the air. The other person's reaction can please you. Someone who has been on friendly terms with you could also have romantic designs.

Friday the 11th. Work appears to be piling up. Get busy and clear it out of the way. You may not have been realistic about what you could accomplish. It may take more time than you thought. Extra effort is likely to be required. Do not allow distractions to get in your way. Co-workers are not likely to be of much help now.

Saturday the 12th. Procrastination would not be wise today. You have some time to prepare for the Christmas holidays. Try not to waste it by puttering around. Careful shopping could put you ahead and help you avoid later crowds. Save the evening for a get-together with loved ones. Someone special may surprise you with an offer.

Sunday the 13th. If you have caught up with errands or shopping, give yourself a break. Friends or family would probably like to see more of you. Take time to give attention to children. Some may need guidance with problems or support in their endeavors. You can set a good example to a partner by restraining spending on impulse items.

Monday the 14th. This looks like a promising and bright new start to the week. There is a likelihood that worries that have been getting you down lately will begin to diminish. This is probably partly because of a change in your perspective. A general increase in confidence should help you to move forward more positively with your plans.

Tuesday the 15th. It could prove exciting to make the most of your creative talents. Possibly you can market a special skill for lucrative results and gain an additional source of income. Focus on starting new enterprises. This is a day when relying more on your own initiative is likely to bring the best results. Make contact with experienced people.

Wednesday the 16th. This should be a sociable and lively day. As the holiday approaches take time for catching up with friends you have not seen for a while. Even if there has been a rift in a relationship, it is likely that enough time has passed for any misunderstandings to be forgotten. A romantic reunion is possible for Scorpio who may have lately split up with someone.

Weekly Summary

You could find your creativity coming to the fore this week. If you make the most of your talents, you can help secure your future. Using your initiative can bear fruit. Make influential people aware of your ambitions. Changing your outlook is bound to boost your confidence. You can move ahead with plans you had put aside for a time.

Do not let a possible upset in a personal relationship throw you. Scorpio likes to be in control where possible. You can be if you handle a situation with forthrightness. Getting in touch with old friends is a cheery way to begin the holidays. Any past problems are likely to be forgotten. A romantic involvement could appear where it is least expected.

Take care to avoid stress and strain this week. You could feel pressured because of the Christmas holidays. Determine to set aside time to begin shopping. Even getting a part of it done will improve your spirits. Do not be tempted to dwell on something you have not accomplished. It may not be that important. Set aside time to relax and enjoy the company of those around you. Be an example to children. Their appreciation of your efforts will be your reward.

51st Week/December 17–23

Thursday the 17th. If you are doing some Christmas shopping today, guard your pocketbook or wallet. Be wary of anyone who bumps into you or tries to get too close. Some Scorpio may be shopping by catalogue. Check the prices carefully and look for the shipping and handling charges. Some things may not be worth the price of sending them. Take time for some fun with a loved one.

Friday the 18th. Today could mark the beginning of a profitable phase where the job is concerned. A promising development is likely to advance your ambitions. If you have been trying for a promotion or raise, someone is backing you. Do not hesitate to make a move. Act quickly while the opportunity is still there.

Saturday the 19th. Rest up and recharge your batteries this weekend. You should be without a long string of commitments to fulfill or engagements to keep. In fact, a little boredom is likely to be the only real problem. If you feel in need of stimulation, make a point of getting in touch with someone congenial. A gossiping neighbor could exhaust your patience.

Sunday the 20th. Try to avoid spending the day on the telephone. This is a time when contacting other people can dig up cans of worms that you might not want to face. Think twice before contacting people who tend to dump all their problems on you. If something is troubling you, do not fret on the matter. Instead, clear your mind by writing your thoughts down.

Monday the 21st. Crossed wires are likely to create a few complications in work or business today. It is to your advantage to go to great lengths to check documents and communications before they are sent out. The more effort you put into attending to details, the less problems you should have to deal with. Aim to be neighborly if a simple favor is asked of you.

Tuesday the 22nd. This should be a day of movement in relation to property matters. Except some good news. A business deal that has been on the brink of conclusion is likely to go forward today. You will probably have a few doubts about whether anything will happen before the day is through, but be patient. Do not necessarily trust someone who tries to make a play for your sympathies.

Wednesday the 23rd. If you have not kept ahead of the rush, you may be on a frantic chase today. Calm down and be practical. You do not have to have exactly the gift you think is right for someone. Shop in one place and look carefully. Should you be hosting festivities, make sure all arrangements are in place.

Weekly Summary

This is a festive week, but not all work or business will come to a halt. A break could come on the work front when you least expect it. It appears that your efforts will come to fruition. Those who are backing you have finally come through. They cannot do everything, however. It is up to you to follow up and use every advantage you have. A complication could arise on the job when communications get fouled up. They can be straightened out but will take more of your time than you would like.

The weekend should be a time to take it easy. You may not have all your holiday shopping done but rushing around is not likely to prove fruitful. Talking to a congenial friend is a good way to spend a pleasant time. Try not to be upset, however, if you run into a problem with someone who wants to pour out all his or her troubles onto you. This is a time to be firm and let others know you have better things to do. Set aside an hour or two to check over holiday arrangements.

To your surprise, you could be in a good position to conclude a business deal. You were probably despairing that anything would ever move forward. Be wary, however, if someone tries to change any details or add conditions. Be firm now that you are on the brink of closing the deal.

52nd Week/December 24–31

Thursday the 24th. Catch up on any backlog before taking off for the holiday. Then you can take a break and enjoy yourself. Accept a social invitation. If possible, ask someone close to accompany you. If you are surrounded by family on this Christmas Eve, take the opportunity to let them know how much you have valued their support through the year.

Friday the 25th. Merry Christmas! This should be a truly delightful Christmas day. You may have more to celebrate than the obvious. Family gatherings are likely to be uplifting through the presence of young visitors. An unexpected romantic opportunity is likely to warm the hearts of single Scorpio. Make a point of calling up someone special.

Saturday the 26th. Try to get involved in the domestic chores today if you are visiting with relatives. If you are the one who is hosting a gathering, you are likely to benefit by accepting offers of help from your guests. The family spirit around you at the moment should be especially heartwarming. Make the most of a chance to be close to loved ones.

Sunday the 27th. This is potentially a rather busy day if you do not repress your desire to please other people. Try to take things fairly easy. The holiday is not quite over for most of you. If you are returning to work tomorrow, it is probably a good idea to make the most of an opportunity for rest and relaxation today. Avoid making frantic, last-minute social arrangements.

Monday the 28th. It is likely that for many of you, this will be a day of throwing yourself full tilt back into work activities. There may be a backlog to catch up on, but try to ease your way in. Do not forget that you still have the rest of the week to deal with. Prepare and organize with the future in mind. Aim to spend some quality time with your partner.

Tuesday the 29th. This should be a good day for catching up on missed-out time with your spouse or romantic partner. If there have been any problems in your relationship lately, it is likely that you will be able to smooth them out. For single Scorpio, this evening looks like a prime time for getting out to meet new people and make renewed contact with friends.

Wednesday the 30th. Business affairs are likely to be slow today. Too many people are unavailable. But you can make this a day of accomplishments. It could be a good time to get things done around the home. Loved ones and friends are probably involved with their own end-of-year plans. You will be able to concentrate without interruptions.

Thursday the 31st. Sending out the old year with festivities and fun is sure to be a happy time for you. Friends and neighbors call or drop in to wish you well. Scorpio may take the time to draw up some New Year's resolutions. If you do, remember they are not written in stone. The new year will be fulfilling if you do your best and let each day be a challenge.

Weekly Summary

You cannot really fail to enjoy yourself with family and friends this week. Gatherings given by neighbors are likely to be especially cordial. If you are alone, do accept that friendly invitation from the people next door. It is likely that they genuinely wish to have you around to celebrate with. For all Scorpio, the younger members of the family are likely to be the source of greatest entertainment this Christmas.

Even though you may be away from work for the holiday, there will most likely still be plenty of tasks to fulfill around the home. If you are doing the entertaining, it is a good idea to elicit help from other family members and friends early on in the proceedings. If you are a guest, be willing to help with the various stacks of washing up that accumulate around a large group of people.

Romance is likely to be in the air. Do not be surprised if you find mistletoe about your head at some point in the festivities. Celebrations taking place at a local bar may well be the jumping off point for you single Scorpio men and women to launch into a new partnership.

DAILY FORECASTS:
JULY–DECEMBER 1997

Tuesday July 1st. Although business finances are flowing reasonably you may have problems over taxes. Certain private deals, especially those involving property, should be kept under wraps a little longer. You may be offered a pay raise or promotion.

Wednesday the 2nd. A lot of work, such as decorating, can be done around the house. Communications are lively and open. Preparing food and games for a family get-together occupies your time happily. Be careful driving and expect delays on the road.

Thursday the 3rd. The morning may be spent on bookkeeping and tax or insurance matters. Later on you may feel like taking a trip with the family. Shopping can be successful, especially if you are buying business equipment. Scorpio has an eagle eye.

Friday the 4th. It is an auspicious time to begin a honeymoon. Someone you meet through a relative may become a new romantic partner. You should find that a private business is suddenly paying off now. But don't bank on it for a steady income.

Saturday the 5th. You seem undecided about taking a proposed trip. It would be wise to discuss the idea further with everyone involved. A decision you make now may have a startling effect on the family. Enjoy exercise and mild sport near home.

Sunday the 6th. Scorpio charm and tact make a hit in the public arena. Performers fare well today. You may launch a publicity campaign to advance a professional goal. Be bold and daring, but not too unconventional or you will set people against your ideas.

Monday the 7th. If it is hard to master the complexities of a second language, study with a teammate. Sympathy toward a needy neighbor may not be enough. He or she may prefer practical aid such as help with the shopping or a lift to the doctor.

Tuesday the 8th. A tax matter is becoming worrisome. Seek expert advice. A political meeting may completely alter your attitudes and values. Be careful you are not being manipulated by a group. Step back if you sense trouble from a rowdy crowd.

Wednesday the 9th. It is a favorable time to consult an important spiritual figure. A group of foreign visitors may effect a real change in your life. Meetings at work help to iron out a lot of problems. But you will have to use persuasion before things go your way.

Thursday the 10th. Your compassion toward a neighbor makes him or her feel better. Just walking through your neighborhood may reveal sights and interests you never knew existed. Community service and philanthropy are accented now.

Friday the 11th. Scorpio public life and private life intertwine nicely today. You will want to help the community or a charity in some way. A brother or sister may reveal an impending separation or divorce. You may be called on to mediate.

Saturday the 12th. This can be a busy day for home entertaining. You may be in the mood to invite a host of people over to your place. But things keep going wrong in lots of silly little ways. Don't let minor annoyances get you down. Lighten up a bit.

Sunday the 13th. Now you are deeply concerned for a near relative's welfare. News of illness or problems in the family will upset you, making you appear vague and anxious. A neighbor will offer sympathy and kindness. Unburden yourself for a change.

Monday the 14th. Be tactful and choose carefully what you say at work today. An unexpected visit or phone call may directly affect your plans. It will take the help of all the family to get a big project going. Using your home for business meetings can be a good move. An older person offers wise advice.

Tuesday the 15th. Today you are likely to be confident about your abilities and powers of persuasion. Still, a lot of tact is needed to reach agreement on a family move. Take care not to be hypocritical. Renovating may be taking place at home. Keep a few secrets when people ask about your busy life.

Wednesday the 16th. A recent change in your home situation may be good for you financially. Carefully designed plans are now paying off. You may decide to work from home. A lot seems to be going on under the surface or behind the scenes. It is not yet time to announce your recent decisions.

Thursday the 17th. This can be a good day for shopping. You may go far afield to find the best sales and bargains in out-of-the-way stores. If you are doing business from home with a lot of entertaining, you may need new clothes for special occasions. Evening favors short pleasure trips.

Friday the 18th. Travel and communications are accented in a positive way. You may see more of your neighbors. Catch up on the gossip. A brother or sister may visit. It is a good time to settle down to correspondence or reading. If you are planning a reunion, send out the invitations now.

Saturday the 19th. Certain old worries surface again and bother you. You may be concerned about the health of an older person. Or mechanical problems arise. Be careful not to mislay messages. A teacher or parent will offer constructive criticism. Don't sulk or storm. Learn from your mistakes.

Sunday the 20th. The morning hours are especially kind to Scorpios of a spiritual inclination. Later in the day a sudden visit from a family friend may alter your plans. But you will find this distraction quite enlivening and cheering. A parent may approach you about an old debt or other money matter.

Monday the 21st. It can be an especially happy day if you are in your home environment. Gardening and construction work are strenuous but rewarding occupations. If you busy yourself with the everyday mundane tasks you will get a lot done. Scorpio is in a disciplined and organized mood now.

Tuesday the 22nd. Early hours favor outlining a financial plan for a creative project. Later you will have to cope with a lover's jealous moods or insensitive behavior. Try not to manipulate people for your own ends. A child may appeal to your emotions in order to wheedle extra allowance out of you.

Wednesday the 23rd. Today's calm conditions favor pursuring a favorite hobby or creative interest. You should be able to enjoy the peace and quiet in your own way. A lover may be in a very caring mood. Children are manageable and will listen to reason. Evening hours are good for filmmakers or moviegoers.

Thursday the 24th. For the Scorpio who is in charge of a business or office, this can be a banner day. Team spirit helps. You may claim some rich rewards for completing neglected tasks. Some of you may buy a pet for your children. Help them learn how to care for it. Your health should be improved.

Friday the 25th. Steady application to a task in hand is the means to accomplish a lot today. You may be irritated by an older person's nagging ways. You are doing very well professionally and can win applause. Still, keep a few secrets. A dinner date tonight may prove to be a fiasco.

Saturday the 26th. A meeting can cause problems for your partner in some way. Someone may resent it if you outshine them in a public forum. You hold your own in an interesting conversation with a group of professionals. In fact, people may be surprised at the store of information you house.

Sunday the 27th. A mate or lover may break a promise today despite your expectations. A hopeful interlude occurs during a conversation. Some Scorpios may deliver a talk on healing techniques or charitable concerns. A forum or town meeting on public health issues can be a real eye-opener.

Monday the 28th. A mislaid letter or neglected phone message can lead to loss or expense. You may have to call a meeting about a financial or business matter. A tax form can be a hassle. A friendly boss can point you toward expert help. Anxiety can tire you. Express your worries and you will feel better.

Tuesday the 29th. Your efforts at expanding a business hit pay dirt. Real estate and other property negotiations are fortunate today. You may sell a house that has been on the market for ages. Increased income will allay recent worries. A reunion of the clan could result in fresh discord and dispute.

Wednesday the 30th. Arrange on short notice to take time off for a trip. Buoyant influences favor travel and study. An exploring urge may lead you to learn a new language or a special craft. Journeys for business purposes go smoothly. Your interest in a relative's welfare will be rewarded.

Thursday the 31st. Buoyant, high spirits continue. Go out for a pleasant sojourn with friends. A day trip to the beach or a night out at a park concert can be most relaxing. A loved one may decide to give you a treat. It is worth traveling a fair distance to enjoy a romantic dinner by candlelight.

Friday August 1st. Auspices change and make travel frustrating today. Cancellations or delays can be the rule rather than the exception. You will be very tired after a long day's journey. You are not in the mood to extend sympathy to a neighbor.

Saturday the 2nd. It's hard to keep to your goals today. If you go about things in a halfhearted way, you cannot count on effecting the desired changes or reforms. There are a few surprises in store for you. Unexpected happenings can upset or throw you.

Sunday the 3rd. This is a favorable day for Scorpios in the public eye. But your attention will be focused more on the home, especially important family gatherings, than on your professional life. Patience will see you through a loved one's health crisis.

Monday the 4th. You may have to make medical arrangements for a loved one. A hitch in your plans will have a domino effect, upsetting the people you live with and work with. Someone may stir up old resentments. Don't let a friend manipulate you.

Tuesday the 5th. Work may be secondary to study activities and social engagements today. Meetings and lectures will be interesting and instructive. Gossiping with friends can be lively but time wasting nonetheless. A relative may invite you out for a treat.

Wednesday the 6th. You will be assessing your chances for realizing certain goals. Right now you feel less stimulated by social events. Friends may keep their distance. Also, little may be going on at work. Take advantage of the lull to forward a pet project.

Thursday the 7th. Scorpio is in a mood to reform a few areas of your life. This can lead you to spiritual paths, a study of the occult, and psychology. You may be involved in research to unearth helpful information. The day is also good for restoration work.

Friday the 8th. You have luck on your side now even though you may encounter some official ineptitude or intervention. Confidently approach an influential person who can help you with a professional matter. A foreign visitor may play a part in your career. You may meet a dignitary or famous actor.

Saturday the 9th. It is a time to write creative prose and read spiritual materials. Some Scorpios will privately nurture certain insights. Perhaps you will receive a promotion or recognition today. But don't become carried away with your own importance. You would make colleagues feel insecure and resentful.

Sunday the 10th. A neighbor may be highly insensitive and make you angry. You will become unduly upset and even consider revenge. But a good talk with a friend can help restore your perspective. Perhaps you are confused about an intimate relationship. This is a time to bring resentments out in the open.

Monday the 11th. This is a delicate day to face a boss about a pay raise or favor. You may need to ask for time off to attend some social function. However, if you employ your tact and charm, you will be able to get your way eventually. A loved one, finding you very hard to please these days, will tell you so.

Tuesday the 12th. Shrewd property moves can put money in your pocket. You seem to have your nose to the ground these days, and can sniff out a good bargain or a sound investment. Going by your hunches is the best way to work as you do believe in your gut feelings. Donate old possessions to charity.

Wednesday the 13th. You will find it hard to persuade a group of business owners to expand their premises or their markets. However, you have the backing and support of key people. Government influence and funds can help. Apply for community assistance if you are dreaming up some development scheme.

Thursday the 14th. Scorpio is ready for some lively debates. It is a good day for physical activities of all kinds. You may want to take part in sailing or a boat race. Your assertive attitude can certainly open doors for you now. This is a good time to make decisions that affect future security.

Friday the 15th. Although you may run up against official problems, you are determined to see a personal plan or project through. Meetings or lectures go well. You may be asked to handle fund-raising for a local charity or community group. A lover can seem very romantic and sensitive tonight.

Saturday the 16th. This is a good day for any healing work or making money for charitable groups. You may join or even lead a sponsored activity for the common good. Take care not to overdo any physical exertions if you are not used to them. Still, you are determined to give your all to a worthy cause.

Sunday the 17th. It is a most auspicious day for family get-togethers. Young and old can enjoy each other's company at a wedding or christening or other celebration. You may have to do a lot of organizing and preparing. But everything should go smoothly. An older person gets a lucky break today.

Monday the 18th. Things at home can be topsy-turvy this morning. You and a parent may not see eye-to-eye. An older child can also prove to be a handful. But you can alter a bad mood by sheer willpower and determination. The afternoon is likely to be enjoyable. Energetic sports can put you in balance.

Tuesday the 19th. It is a day when romantic relationships are sure to flourish. A quiet, tender meeting with a lover in a private place is indicated. You can feel very deeply and intensely about each other. Some private creative work may pay you a good dividend. You will enjoy writing and composing music.

Wednesday the 20th. Morning hours favor composing or teaching music and song writing. If you are handling other people's money, do not get involved in risky or offbeat money-making schemes. A love affair is mounting in intensity. Do not rush headlong into a premature commitment.

Thursday the 21st. Be disciplined and orderly in whatever you pursue today. Once the mundane activities are completed, you are free to resume a creative pastime. Co-workers are jovial and good-tempered. Someone may give you a fine idea for a new project. Stay alert in sports to avert possible injury.

Friday the 22nd. Some Scorpios may be recuperating from a minor injury or mild illness. A boss can be very sympathetic toward your needs and problems. When neighbors ask for a favor, you may not be prepared to help out. If a partner is cranky, you may fly into a rage. Take extra care to prevent an accident.

Saturday the 23rd. An honest talk with a partner will go a long way in reaching an understanding. But don't expect miracles. You still may feel shaken. Talking things through with a friend or counselor will provide a detached viewpoint and give you some perspective. It is an accident-prone time, so slow down.

Sunday the 24th. The morning may see a change of heart between you and a mate or lover. You can feel compassionate and contrite. Now an air of forgiveness flows all around you. Early hours also favor spiritual talks and meetings. Later there is the possibility of trouble arising with a leader in your group.

Monday the 25th. Negotiating business and financial agreements is the order of the day. Be firm if a meeting becomes unmanageable. A group of young people may be giving you a hard time today. A guided tour to some interesting art galleries, museums, and showplaces would keep the students occupied.

Tuesday the 26th. It is easier now to negotiate agreements and to settle tax and insurance claims. An official will be on your side. Research should proceed well, and you will enjoy delving into old diaries, ledgers, manuscripts, and other records. An older person may be helpful in a money matter.

Wednesday the 27th. This favorable day is perfect for beginning a journey or vacation. Scorpio is confident and in the peak of good health. You will enjoy spirited conversations and may be introduced to an important person. Help youngsters and young adults master their studies and special interests.

Thursday the 28th. If you travel for any reason, you may feel burdened and fatigued. An older person may not be up to a trip. If you have to see an elderly in-law who is ailing, phone instead of visiting. Some Scorpios may begin to doubt long-held beliefs. Do not give in to negative thinking.

Friday the 29th. Disillusionment or loss may make you sad and depressed. Scorpio travelers may find that a vacation resort isn't all it's chalked up to be. Make the most of what you have. Family and friends can be more important than ever now. Confide in them. Self-expression is good for the soul.

Saturday the 30th. A work situation can get out of hand if you don't keep an eye on it. It may be that everyone is gossiping and goofing off instead of getting down to the business at hand. A parent or family member may arouse your anger. But in the end good sense and loving feelings will prevail.

Sunday the 31st. Being absorbed with your duties and daily tasks keeps your mind off problems and worries. You are in an organized mood and can get a lot done. But don't be troubled if you go slowly. Rushing could spoil it. Church and community meetings fare well. An influential person is on your side.

Monday September 1st. A goal may be realized now. Your message will be heard in any talks or lectures you give. Group activities and community meetings go well. You have a lot of clout among friends. An important move can be made on a business venture, which opens the door to opportunity.

Tuesday the 2nd. Health becomes paramount now. A sudden sore throat or cold may stop you from doing all your work. You may need to stay in bed. If the situation persists, you will have to spend a good deal on doctor's fees or medicine. A parent or boss may be difficult, and your lover seems indifferent.

Wednesday the 3rd. Your interest in healing or spiritual matters can produce very good ideas for helping people less fortunate. You may begin a unique neighborhood outreach program. A friend may reveal intriguing secrets. Use key information to advance your private money accounts.

Thursday the 4th. This calm day favors work on home renovation and improvement schemes. A lover will make you feel happy now. Be careful that a secret meeting is not found out. A friend or relative may not be trustworthy, so do not rely on them.

Friday the 5th. Discrimination and discretion are required if you are trying to keep a secret. Act judiciously, as luck is not on your side now. A visit to a loved one in the hospital can be quite depressing. A lover may be rejecting or distant. There may be an actual separation. Even you may be cooling down toward someone you once adored.

Saturday the 6th. Original and unusual schemes and ideas can be proposed, and key people will be convinced. You are highly inventive and well-informed about your subject. Some Scorpios may be drawn to study astrology, perhaps even teaching it. Gatherings in your home can prove most interesting.

Sunday the 7th. Leading a group can demand quick but intelligent decisions. Be principled and refuse to use your ability to speak well as a means of power or manipulation. Be open to other viewpoints as well. The words of another influential person can really move you. You must take a stand.

Monday the 8th. Although a mate or lover's absence can be stressful, Scorpio ably handles relationship problems with sensitivity and compassion. You will find the courage to share an important idea or plan with the family, especially a parental figure. Nourish the secret hope in your heart.

Tuesday the 9th. Managing the finances of a professional group may lead to a few problems with one of its influential members. But maintain a sense of humor and keep your wits. Perseverance and dogged attention to detail can help settle any problems. A notice from an official requires a prompt answer.

Wednesday the 10th. Indications today are fine for solving your cash flow shortage. You can make some money for charity and enjoy yourself at the same time. When a loved one buys you a gift, you are likely to value the thought above all. Get together with neighbors to discuss some local problem.

Thursday the 11th. Instead of wasting time on gossip, attack neglected chores. You can catch up on correspondence, phone calls, or duty visits of various kinds. Fulfill an obligation to a neighbor. Shopping is likely to be in your immediate vicinity. Get a head start on this term's studies by reading all you can.

Friday the 12th. Creativity flows for the Scorpio in music, photography, and filmmaking. But keep track of the details of your work so that nothing goes wrong. Be alert for errors. Red tape may prevent you from fulfilling your daily schedule. You are not in the mood to brook such interference.

Saturday the 13th. Things may not turn out today as you planned, but chance events can be even better than your initial hopes. For that reason have trust when a family member suggests an alternative scheme. You will enjoy a meeting to discuss philosophy and religion and exciting new ventures.

Sunday the 14th. It is a good time to tackle some complicated repair work at home. The day also favors intense creative effort. For Scorpios doing volunteer or charity work, the sense of duty well done can give great satisfaction. Control your impulses when dealing with narrow-minded individuals.

Monday the 15th. It is a fine day for Scorpio in love. You should be at your most charming and attractive. You feel good and look good. It may be hard to keep your mind on a concert or other performance this evening if you are thinking about your lover. Gossip and intrigue will be annoying.

Tuesday the 16th. It is a happy day in many ways, but you can wind up feeling upset about a personal matter. Scorpio is filled with idealism. When you throw yourself into the fray, a friend or a group leader may put your back up. Do not challenge authority figures. You might alienate them.

Wednesday the 17th. Home repairs and renovations may be going on for some Scorpios. Your daily routine may be disrupted by such work. The team spirit is high among colleagues at regular work and business. If you are involved in an important project or study together, things can go very well today.

Thursday the 18th. This tricky day poses some difficulties. Work will be a drag, as your concentration tends to waver. Someone in business may be trying to pull the wool over your eyes about a certain matter. If you feel ill, the reason may be emotional rather than physical. A pet may need special care.

Friday the 19th. Use tact to settle an argument with a partner. Don't try out too many practical jokes on the family. They may get most upset and retaliate. This is a good day for clothes shopping and beauty treatments. Looking and feeling glamorous and attractive, you can make a powerful impact.

Saturday the 20th. Try to keep your cool when faced with a partner's aggravating ways. You may be ready to blow your top at the slightest upset, but such rage can hardly help the situation. Show sensitivity and deal with people charitably. You seldom forget a grudge. But cast revenge from your heart and learn to forgive.

Sunday the 21st. Trying to outmaneuver someone over a financial deal may not work. Check the facts and figures before you act. A family business may be in need of expansion. But this is not the time for making a move. Matters outside your control will frustrate your initial plan. Revise your strategy.

Monday the 22nd. Use logic and common sense to get things organized. The details of a financial matter can be sorted out. Be hesitant about putting private funds into a corporate situation. You may be taking too much of a risk. Try not to wear your heart on your sleeve in a new love affair.

Tuesday the 23rd. Stay alert on this uneasy day. You may be starting a new course of study and finding everything strange and unfamiliar. Travelers can be thwarted by hidden factors. Plan some alternative routes for your journey and be on the safe side. A child may be acting secretively.

Wednesday the 24th. It's a fine day for enjoying a trip to some scenic spot. Take time off to visit galleries and museums in your area. Learn more about art and architecture. The Scorpio abroad should be able to capture some romantic moments. Your personal magnetism is sure to draw people to you.

Thursday the 25th. A lighthearted, romantic mood prevails. But you may be in for some kind of disappointment while traveling. If you feel very tired this morning, it will be hard to get organized for a trip. But you shake off the lethargy and will become confident. A child can be very important to you today.

Friday the 26th. Keep in touch with loved ones and friends. Scorpios at work and in business may be expecting too much. Be realistic. If you promise more than you can deliver, you will be courting trouble. An influential person can be most helpful, though you may not realize it until later.

Saturday the 27th. This is a quiet day on the work and business scene. Home life, though, is lively. The family may be planning a surprise. You may find that an unconventional figure in your life becomes more important. A child in the hospital will take a turn for the better, a cause to celebrate.

Sunday the 28th. Plans for sport or entertainment may have to be put aside due to unforeseen circumstances. Money may give you a headache. A wedding or other celebration can be expensive business. Reconsider the arrangements. Be entirely scrupulous if you are managing other people's funds.

Monday the 29th. Close relationships are tender and intense. You do seem inclined to please people now. Such affability certainly makes you more popular. Enjoy a massage or beauty treatment. Select a new outfit with some jewelry to enhance the effect. A party may signal a new romance for some of you.

Tuesday the 30th. Many Scorpios feel strongly about your ideals and beliefs, and say so vehemently. A charitable group you belong to may choose you as their spokesperson. You are a good deal more assertive than usual these days. A wish may come true tonight. Celebrate a promising new partnership.

Wednesday October 1st. This is sure to be a most rewarding day. You may spend it peacefully at home in the privacy of your den. It often suits the Scorpio temperament to be alone for a while. Today you can philosophize, contemplate, and just be yourself.

Thursday the 2nd. Share your religious convictions and spiritual feelings with family and friends. Gift giving is a joy. Visit a loved one in the hospital, or do charitable work. Someone from your past may contact you. It hardly makes a ripple on your calm ocean.

Friday the 3rd. Your mood is restless and ready for action. A sudden event at home gets you worked up. You may find that a property deal is not going through as easily as you hoped. Try not to manipulate a money deal. Let things be and trust people.

Saturday the 4th. Scorpio will be champing at the bit today. Family members find your moods extreme and may tell you so. There is a tendency to be careless about certain matters. If you have put on weight recently, it may bother you now.

Sunday the 5th. You are set to make a conquest today. There is no doubt you look glamorous, sexy, and enchanting. Work your magic, and no one can resist your charms. A relaxed air suits you in your pursuit of love. But be sensitive to people's needs.

Monday the 6th. A phone call today may solve a business problem. A private, behind-the-scenes deal may work out in your favor. Be ready to seize any opportunities to make extra money on the side. Someone could be helping you without your knowing it.

Tuesday the 7th. Reading and study are favored this slow day. If your work is usually connected with property, banking, or other big money schemes, review your accounts. Sort through your possessions and see what you can donate to charity.

Wednesday the 8th. A devil-may-care attitude will delight a lover. Enjoy your present lighthearted mood. Plans for altering or expanding the home can keep you happy. A distant member of the family may phone and offer you some concrete help, perhaps a loan. Evening is good for reading and study.

Thursday the 9th. An elderly person may be ailing today and need a lot of attention. You will be busy with doctors and hospitals for a while. Although these duties can seem burdensome at times, you are able to get yourself and others organized. Take care traveling. Do not speed and risk getting a ticket.

Friday the 10th. You will be implementing a few changes around the house today. Schemes for beautifying the place can keep you busy. You can also spend time organizing the closets and clearing out unwanted items, especially clothes. Responsibility for the welfare of an aging family member weighs on you.

Saturday the 11th. Working methodically through your daily tasks and activities helps, and you will get your affairs in order by midday. Call in an expert to fix machinery that may be giving you trouble. Make sure that you or a mechanic has thoroughly checked a car, or you may be left stranded.

Sunday the 12th. Unforeseen events indicate a change in the plans you made for today. Sudden meetings can be exciting and stimulating. Keep things spontaneous rather than too controlled and tight. Then you really can have some fun. A lover may be possessive and demanding. Your feelings are also intense.

Monday the 13th. A child can tell you some amusing tales today. You, in turn, will be a witty and helpful guide to a group of youngsters. Reading to someone who is sick or in bed can really cheer them up. You are in the mood to learn as well as teach. Being creative gives you great joy.

Tuesday the 14th. The Scorpio ability to handle large sums of money will be useful at work today. Managing wage or tax matters can keep you busy. Some unexpected occurrences demand all your wily skills. The day favors teamwork in study and research. Explore new therapies and alternative medicines.

Wednesday the 15th. Health and fitness concerns come to the fore. You may be on a diet. If so, take vitamin pills and rest periodically. You may be feeling tired, even a bit down at times. Your daily routine could be getting boring and thankless. Try to be positive and more gregarious. Visit a friend.

Thursday the 16th. A partner is not seeing things your way about a family matter. Other loved ones also express opposing points of view. This calls for a compromise. But no one is in the mood to give in. A friend may prove most unreliable. Some machinery you ordered for the house may be faulty.

Friday the 17th. Show sensitivity toward a partner's moods and attitudes. It is no use acting superior. A recent deception may come out into the open, causing hurt feelings and untoward reactions. Be straightforward with a neighbor. You now are highly imaginative, or just inclined to fantasize.

Saturday the 18th. Today you are capable of talking your way out of any trouble or misunderstanding. Some of you will be inclined to delve into occult or mystical happenings. Your interest in making money may send you to secondhand stores. Scorpios enjoy recycling junk and generally do well at it.

Sunday the 19th. Now you can profit from branching out and being more expansive. You have a new venture all worked out and organized. Do not exhaust yourself trying to please people. Entertaining at home can be successful. Continue your efforts to make the place look attractive and welcoming.

Monday the 20th. A bank manager, accountant, or lawyer can be most helpful to you behind the scenes. You will need solid professional advice tucked under your belt when tackling a property negotiation. A meeting held abroad or in some distant venue should go well. You may be asked to take the chair.

Tuesday the 21st. Traveling will not be much fun today. You are likely to be held up by traffic jams, faulty machinery, possibly even a strike. Be sure your passport, tickets, and other travel documents are in order. Officials can be very fussy, checking even the smallest detail. Be prepared.

Wednesday the 22nd. Unfamiliar territory can pose problems for the Scorpio traveler. Be sure to have a reliable guide or a good map. A secret meeting with a legal representative can make you anxious. You may not have facts to back up your case. A student may try to deceive you.

Thursday the 23rd. Recent changes will eventually benefit your business and professional life. Still, it can take time to adjust to new routines or ideas. Now that your birthday period begins, you may react to stress in a tense and irritable way. Calm down and learn how to use new technology.

Friday the 24th. Job training will be a plus now. Work goes smoothly if you are disciplined. Co-workers are pulling their weight and helping to get things in order. You may surprise everyone by the mountains you can move today. Study group are enjoyable. What's more, you earn while you learn.

Saturday the 25th. Your plans for recreation and entertainment may be frustrated by circumstances beyond your control. That doesn't mean all is lost. Take a positive approach and come up with an alternative. Lately you are very confident. Being yourself without pretenses can win friends and influence people.

Sunday the 26th. Your ability to communicate what you feel can take you a long way. You have developed positive habits and values. A loved one will show warmth and affection. The day favors group activities. You may lead a debate or chair a meeting. The Scorpio performer will be successful.

Monday the 27th. Service to the community in general and especially to your neighborhood is indicated today. You can help people less fortunate than yourself by writing an article, taking door-to-door collections, or distributing leaflets. Later you may become restless. A short trip or visit would be in order.

Tuesday the 28th. A money shortage looms on the horizon. Stop spending and start budgeting. Perhaps you can find extra work to increase your income. Secrets weigh on you and must be unburdened. A family friend or doctor may be the best person to see. Special research may take you to unusual places.

Wednesday the 29th. Today you will be very busy juggling a varied work load. Scorpios who work in hospitals may find elderly folk especially demanding. Use tact in a tricky situation with an official. You will exert yourself tirelessly in order to raise money for charity. A loved one can be giving and intense.

Thursday the 30th. Trouble will ensue if you hide anything from a relative. A neighbor may call asking for help. Be sure you are doing the right thing and not being played for a sucker. You may be tense and upset later. Problems with machinery may mean having to rush out and buy a necessary item.

Friday the 31st. Tackle troublesome concerns. Problems at home or with a young family member may be exaggerated. Be sure you have all the facts right before preaching or laying down the law. You may behave in a slightly careless or hypocritical manner today. Try not to overdo the parental role.

Saturday November 1st. A sensitive and caring approach is the right note for today. Your need to be helpful can lead you to join a local issue or cause. Teachers and students reach a good rapport. Tutoring a youngster can earn you money on the side. Music and photography can also be sources of extra income.

Sunday the 2nd. The Scorpio imagination continues active and profitable. Unique money-making ventures are indicated. Follow your intuition and gamble on a hunch. Deal swiftly with tax or insurance matters. A friend may be able to answer any tricky questions. A parent can be very generous now.

Monday the 3rd. It is a quiet day for Scorpios in banking, money markets, and real estate. Catch up on personal bookkeeping. Think up ways to earn extra cash or ways to improve savings and investments. Also, decide whether you really need all the possessions you have collected over the years.

Tuesday the 4th. This lively day favors efforts to earn extra money or to increase your capital. Spend cautiously if you go shopping with a loved one. Plenty of birthday gifts will be coming your way. People close to you feel generous and want to shower you with presents. A party or dinner date will be fun.

Wednesday the 5th. Many Scorpios are now playing a leading role in the community. You will be very sympathetic toward a particular neighborhood cause, especially if it concerns local education issues. Volunteer work requires some sacrifice if family and professional commitments are heavy.

Thursday the 6th. Your ability to help a neighbor can make you feel good in yourself. Pressure to unravel a confused situation may lead you to write or phone an official. Later today you will be in the mood for a family outing. Go shopping together or simply enjoy a scenic drive. Do some work outdoors.

Friday the 7th. This can turn out to be a satisfying day. You should be able to get through your daily tasks in an organized and efficient manner. There will be free time left to take a short trip with a loved one. You may meet an interesting foreign visitor who promotes a deeper understanding of life.

Saturday the 8th. Travel will forward Scorpio interests on this lively day. You may be involved in property negotiations this morning, which probably will turn out to your advantage. A snap decision may be required about a family matter. A child's education will prove to be expensive and demanding.

Sunday the 9th. You will enjoy the theater. If you are an actor, it is a favorable time for a performance. Children look to you for a treat. You can combine sound instruction with fun recreation. Creative efforts take you closer to a goal. Scorpio is capable of producing original work now.

Monday the 10th. Creative inspiration is accented this morning. Enjoy spiritual music or a film in the early hours. Later, the demands of work or home life press on you. An immediate crisis claims your attention and may mean running all over town. Be careful if you are driving, especially after dark.

Tuesday the 11th. If you get up early and buckle down to your routine tasks, you will earn time free later. Then you and the family may enjoy a trip to the countryside. Scorpios at work will feel easier and less burdened. A friendly conversation with a co-worker can lead to a commercial partnership.

Wednesday the 12th. A conflict of interest at work creates a sticky situation. Watch what you say to a co-worker. Misunderstandings will occur if you are tactless. You may feel ill or fatigued. A dreamy attitude does not make the day pass easily. Relax and rest tonight. There are limits to your endurance.

Thursday the 13th. Encouraging words from a mate or lover can really cheer you up. Do not put on a hypocritical act with a relative or neighbor. A business partner may have some new scheme for making extra money. Be sure it's not farfetched or too ambitious, and also be sure it's legitimate.

Friday the 14th. Petty squabbles with a partner over a purely emotional issue can ruin plans for the day. Keep a sense of humor, and soon the matter can be set straight. Mutual efforts to improve home and work situations are favored. You are less inclined to be careless and more inclined to compromise.

Saturday the 15th. It will not be easy to settle an inheritance. People will challenge every detail, and you may have to haggle over every penny. A foreign visitor could come up with some good ideas to improve your business. Be sure your accounts are in perfect order. After a slow start property negotiations take off.

Sunday the 16th. Make the most of a quiet day by relaxing and resting. For some Scorpios this can be a time for deep thinking and decision making. You may be reconsidering a business partnership or devising ways to earn money. Mixed emotions cloud a romantic relationship. Think it through.

Monday the 17th. If traveling is on your agenda today, you may not enjoy the trip. Do not speed, or you could be in trouble. Impulsive and hasty actions can lead to accidents. Some good news about a specialized training course will make you feel better. Test results indicate that you are the perfect candidate for a job.

Tuesday the 18th. If you postponed a trip until today, you were wise. This is a fairly smooth day for travel. Transport problems should be nil. Relatives, especially in-laws, may pay you a visit. Study pursuits proceed slowly, perhaps lacking the challenge Scorpio needs. Help your co-workers complete a task.

Wednesday the 19th. If you can make certain reforms at work, you will improve everyone's efficiency and productivity. Unused or unwanted machinery can be a problem. Your confidence and helpfulness impress a superior. But you could be cold and distant to a neighbor or sibling.

Thursday the 20th. Don't overdo things at work today. You may be upset over an official inquiry. Or you can exaggerate certain problems. Your efficiency works well in most areas. But you may be too confident and thus careless in other areas. Keep an eye on the details of legal and property issues.

Friday the 21st. Try not to challenge an authority figure though you feel you are within your rights. Someone's bad behavior is no excuse for you to go on the warpath. People can feel threatened by Scorpio's show of power, however subtly you wield it. If a child interferes with your schedule, be kind.

Saturday the 22nd. This may turn out to be an emotionally upsetting day. You are ready to flare up at the littlest thing. But if someone is trying to manipulate you, your reaction will be swift. Take care not to let jealousy or suspicion come between you and a dear friend. Gossip and hearsay may be false.

Sunday the 23rd. It is not a good time to hold a meeting about a financial matter. Wait before signing any contracts or agreements. You may not want to attend a function or give a talk today. But it can't hurt just to sit and listen. If a brother or sister is bored, encourage him or her to join you in a game.

Monday the 24th. A bit of secret diplomacy can advance a financial negotiation. Be quick to arrange an interview with a bank manager or lawyer to settle an inheritance. Call a meeting to be held in private. Scorpio will be interested in studying occult matters in a group. Meditation can be transforming.

Tuesday the 25th. You may be in a rush to get through your usual routine today. You want to be free to attend an important family get-together later. Or you may intend to meet a lover at some pleasant rendezvous. A budding new partnership makes you thoughtful but also happy.

Wednesday the 26th. A longing to escape from life's humdrum realities can grip you most of the day. For some Scorpios yoga and meditation will fill the bill. For others, watching a film will mirror your own private dreamworld. Try to be constructive. Do some writing. Expand your knowledge by reading.

Thursday the 27th. Despite a restless urge, you may sit still for this Thanksgiving holiday even though you feel uncomfortable. Maybe you really do need a change of scenery. Moving house, changing a job, even changing partners may be ideas in your mind now. You can be a powerhouse negotiating a financial deal.

Friday the 28th. On this pleasant day Scorpio is sure to be in a charming and even-tempered mood. People are drawn to you when you exude a rare air of sweetness. The day favors shopping for clothes or special diet foods. It will be exciting to imagine a complete change of style and image.

Saturday the 29th. This period continues favorable for making a new start. Keep negotiating financial deals, both personal and business. You may be able to shift stock that has shown little growth. An influential character you meet now will have a profound impact on your life. Be open to change.

Sunday the 30th. Although there may be a slow start to the day, things will liven up later. Make decisions about moving some investments around. Tackle neglected chores around the house and garden. Study is favored in your free time. An elderly person in your care responds to your healing touch.

Monday December 1st. This lively day promotes good communication with people. You will be more active than usual in your local area. Several errands, shopping trips, and visits to neighbors will occupy the time. Nervous energy keeps you on the go.

Tuesday the 2nd. Another busy day is likely to be tiring. A lot of running around can result in a tension headache by the end of the day. Be careful, as you may be prone to chills or falls. Try to slow the pace if possible. A pet may be ill and cause worry.

Wednesday the 3rd. It is a favorable day for Scorpios in art, music, or film. You will be very inspired. Caring for people makes you feel good. The tender words of a loved one can move you deeply. For some Scorpios, a lover may pop the question today.

Thursday the 4th. You can start to make a few changes in the daily running of your life. A group may meet in your home to discuss fund-raising. You will be expected to take the lead. Someone of influence can surprise you with a gift.

Friday the 5th. Make arrangements in anticipation of the festivities ahead. A child can show unusual maturity. You are happy to help an elderly person who falls ill. At work a boss may give you more responsibility, but with extra pay soon to follow.

Saturday the 6th. Theater productions will require additional funds. Do not cut corners in an effort to lower the costs. Maybe you need new investors. A child may try to wangle extra allowance from you. Don't get involved in power battles over money.

Sunday the 7th. It is a good day for creative activities. An injection of funds will guarantee that the play or the concert goes on. A sense of spiritual joy and beauty makes you feel transformed. Love letters from a partner are bright and cheerful.

Monday the 8th. Transport problems arise just when you need to go shopping. But someone is on hand to rescue you. A call from a loved one makes this a special day. Romantic fantasies keep you on cloud nine. And your ability to concentrate on business or study vanishes. People will waste time gossiping.

Tuesday the 9th. A boss may give you a bonus or a pay raise today. This is a good time for getting along with people at work. You may decide to entertain a crowd at your home. Even though this means a lot of arranging and expense, you feel generous and expansive, ready to cope with any challenge.

Wednesday the 10th. Shared activities and joint ventures are favored today. Sit down with a mate to iron out a family problem. It is a good time to write cards and letters. Thinking of people can make you dwell on the past. A nostalgic mood may distract you from daily tasks. Ask a partner or friend to help.

Thursday the 11th. Scorpio should be feeling very happy in a special relationship now. You may go overboard being generous, but such a gesture will be reciprocated. Debates and political rallies stimulate your imagination. You may be rushing around trying to drum up support for a local cause.

Friday the 12th. The morning can be a drag, but things perk up considerably later in the day. Looking at your bank account may be a horrifying prospect now. But sudden windfalls will soon make things look rosier. You may hear some good news from a family member. A party can lead to a romantic interlude.

Saturday the 13th. Money in the mail may finally arrive. Now you can see an official about an accounting problem. An older person's fussiness makes you bad-tempered at times. But you can cope with the extra pressure. Family finances are better organized despite some recent expenditures.

Sunday the 14th. A phone call may put all your plans and schemes for the day on hold. A brother or sister may be acting in a juvenile fashion. Watch out for a tendency to be jumpy and nervous today. Be careful when discussing money matters. Someone close to you is not above telling tales out of school.

Monday the 15th. Daily travel can be disrupted by cancellations or official action. Plans for longer journeys may be held up. On this tiring and heavy day little gets done. There is no point in fighting it. Just give in. Or take the day off work if you can. It will be hard to concentrate on your studies.

Tuesday the 16th. On this complex and confused day you are uncertain what you really want to do. This can mean frittering away your time. An exam may be very hard to follow. Behind-the-scene maneuvers at work keep you in suspense. Even home life lacks harmony. At days's end you feel tired and irritable.

Wednesday the 17th. It can be very hard to stick to any kind of routine today. Sudden events may disrupt plans made by the family. But you can pull things together again. You come to the aid of a friend. If you are working with a team, things can get a bit tricky when one of the members pulls out.

Thursday the 18th. It seems that you have been too optimistic about a property matter. Maybe you have expanded too fast in a career or professional situation. Careless mistakes can create some havoc in your finances. Call your accountant. Speaking another language will impress a foreign visitor.

Friday the 19th. You may feel as if you are being coerced into going somewhere against your will. An outing may be too expensive or include people you do not like. You may try to manipulate a friend by resorting to a little emotional blackmail. This strategy can misfire. Be more straightforward.

Saturday the 20th. It is a difficult day for communicating with people about money. Be wary of con artists and other tricky characters if you go shopping. Keep receipts and bills. Your car can prove unreliable. A group meeting may reveal hidden conflicts and enemies waiting to oppose you.

Sunday the 21st. This morning you can enjoy a wonderful musical or theatrical production. It may be an amateur effort, but it is nevertheless moving and inspirational. If someone in the local area is interfering with your private life, why not call a meeting of neighbors to discuss and combat the problem?

Monday the 22nd. You may find that a member of the family is suddenly taken ill. You are likely to feel quite tired at times today. Try to rest at frequent intervals. Some Scorpios will be busy decorating the house to make things fresh and attractive for visitors. Having people over can provide much cheer.

Tuesday the 23rd. The day favors private get-togethers and select gatherings. You can really enjoy yourself. Maybe someone else is doing the honors for once and giving you a rest. Your mood is expansive and generous. A philosophical attitude about the past enables you to get over some sad memories.

Wednesday the 24th. Scorpio radiates confidence and sunshine today. The family can be very loving and lively. An impromptu party develops when neighbors stop by to visit. One in particular may be special to you now. You are ready for the excitement Hanukkah and Christmas Eve have in store.

Thursday the 25th. Merry Christmas! Your vitality and intensity seem to energize everyone around you. On this day for making merry, you waste no time celebrating the joys of life. As you count your blessings, you are mindful of people less fortunate than you. They will benefit from your generosity.

Friday the 26th. You take great pleasure in seeing your plans work out and everyone having fun. Sports and recreation are favored. Everyone will enjoy exercise, games, walks, and other physical activities. Interesting conversations and news keep things lively. Your feelings of affection and love run high.

Saturday the 27th. Today should prove quite pleasant even if you are back at work. Letters about money matters can be very cheering. An older person may have some good news for you. You may be writing down next year's resolutions. A sense of duty keeps you occupied with business or study.

Sunday the 28th. This should turn out to be a very cheerful and positive day. You can spend some time buying items at a do-it-yourself store. You may be in the mood to continue decorating or improving the place in which you live. You may keep open house and welcome visitors from near and far.

Monday the 29th. When you accidentally encounter an interesting neighbor, you are surprised by a cool reception. You experience a critical attitude as very offputting. A new boss could be a strict disciplinarian. Rigid rules and regulations really stifle you and make it hard to develop bright ideas. Be patient.

Tuesday the 30th. On this erratic day some disillusionment creeps in. Your efforts to work do not succeed, and you end up daydreaming. A desire to escape an unpleasant situation may send you on a journey. Driving to the shore can be healing. Or a good read can transport your imagination.

Wednesday the 31st. It is a splendid day on which to end the old year. You are content to enjoy parties and festivities in your own home. Sum up the past and count your blessings. Loved ones are very special to you now. After a lot of trials, you know where the best things in life can be found.